Havana

Footprint

Caroline Lascom & Sarah Cameron

Contents

Listings

About the authors

Caroline Lascom graduated from Manchester University with a degree in Latin American Studies. After stints at BBC Magazines in London and Evans & Novak in Washington DC, she finally traded the suit for the sarong and got back to her Latin roots. Travelling around Cuba, and Central and South America, she worked as a horseback tour guide in Costa Rica, studied Latin American literature, and the finer points of *capoeira* and *caipirinha* in Brazil, and worked as an English teacher in Argentina. Moving from the wild west lands of the Gaucho to the fantasy world of Gaudí, she then worked as freelance writer and translator in Barcelona before joining the Footprint editorial team, in Bath. Then finally, months, and many *mojitos,* later came the Footprint guide to Havana...

After a degree in Latin American Studies **Sarah Cameron** has been travelling and writing on the continent ever since, both as an economist and as an author for Footprint Handbooks. Initially moonlighting for the South American Handbook in her spare time, in 1990 she parted company with the world of finance and has been contributing to the expansion of Footprint titles ever since. Sarah now concentrates solely on the Caribbean and is the author of the Cuba Handbook, now in its third edition. When she is not travelling around the Caribbean sampling beaches and rum cocktails, she retreats to her 17th-century farmhouse in rural Suffolk.

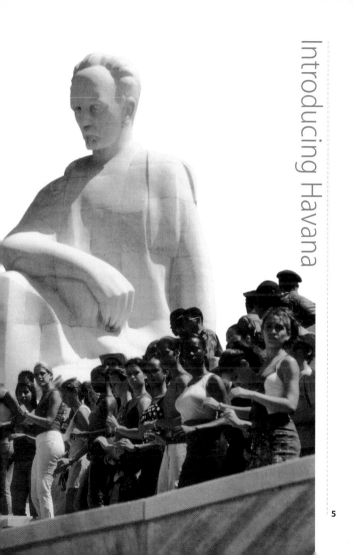

Fidel's island fortress is a mind-blowing place. It's like travelling in a malfunctioning time machine where centuries merge and cultures and ideologies mingle. 1950s American cars lumber alongside horsedrawn carriages, swiftly overtaken by bright yellow egg shells on wheels. Sleek, art deco towers flank whimsical colonial mansions, tourists splurge on US$6 cocktails in palatial hotels, while habaneros gossip in the ration shop queues. American culture is all but outlawed, yet one of Cuba's most lucrative exports is an American literary suicide.

Havana has been a pleasure zone since the 1920s when US neocolonialism injected its own brand of indulgence. A not so holy alliance of gambling, rum and sensuality lured America's thirsty exiles from the Prohibition years. Movie stars and mobsters came to unleash their fantasies and angst-ridden literati pitched up at bars to muse and booze. The cocktail industry boomed with the influx of flashy bartenders, suddenly on the dole Stateside. Rum wizardry culminated in the mojito, adored by Hemingway, now the signature tourist tipple.

Talkin' about the Revolution

With the Revolution, out went Uncle Sam, fetish and free wheeler-dealing, and in came the beret-clad Messiah. While Fidel shuns the cult of personality, the image of Che is everywhere, from revolutionary slogans to steel sculptures and tourist market tat. At the pinnacle of Cuba's revolutionary pantheon is José Martí, who dedicated his life to bringing about the end of Spanish colonial rule. His pen definitely proved mightier than his sword. His much admired poems "*Versos sencillos*", are now more famously rebranded as the song *Guantánamera*.

Sensual healing

Havana is not for the inhibited. In a city where Big Brother is always watching, music and sex are the sacred means to freedom of expression. Music pumps into every nook and cranny, from the Grammy-winning home-grown talent of Los Van Van to The Beatles, and the hip hop of the *roquero* youth. The bodies of lithe young women and muscular men gyrate through the streets. And, when it comes to flirting, *habaneros* take the Oscar. With the wiggle of a hip, the toss of the hair and and the coo coo of the *piropo*, the locals engage freely. Appearance is everything. *Habaneros* struggle to make ends meet but nails get filed, lips are puckered, hair is curled and pooches get pampered. And, while their dwellings slouch into rubble-strewn alleyways, residents still dust off the ornaments, polish their antiques and surgically scrub the floors.

Urban hymns

Havana's not short on A-list attractions with galleries, museums and architecture. The city's heterogenous history has spawned vices, ingrained new ideologies and created iconic legends, leaving in its wake a volatile, but compelling landscape. Sights aside, Havana's enigmatic allure lies in engaging with *habanero* life, wandering into crooked streets or ambling along coastal esplanades, partaking of three of Cuba's essential ingredients: rum, rumba and revelry.

At a glance

La Habana Vieja

Habana Vieja is the epicentre of tourist activity, a labyrinth of alleyways, bulging with architectural splendours, cultural attractions and all manner of pleasure, decadent and divine. This is Havana's colonial heart, where the capital was founded in 1519 on Plaza de Armas, the city's most animated square. A vibrant colonial port, Havana's commercial prowess is still visible in the forts and the remains of the city walls, built to shield Havana's silver booty en route to Spain. As the Marxists were more intent on saving the soul of the nation after the Revolution, the old town's sumptuous colonial mansions and ancient palaces were reduced to sepulchral shells, shored up by wooden crutches. Designated a World Heritage Site in 1982, restoration work is breathing life and, arguably, a banal homogeneity.

Havana Centro

Not the prettiest of districts, and with no real 'must see' sights, Havana Centro is usually dismissed by tourists en route to more aesthetically pleasing areas of the city. Paseo del Prado technically marks Centro's boundary with La Habana Vieja. This serene, tree-lined boulevard was originally outside the city walls, but soon became the heart of the city's social life, a place for Sunday drives, promenades and carnival processions. The walls were demolished after 1863 and construction of the first luxury hotel, the *Sevilla*, took 28 years to complete before it opened in 1908. Where El Prado ends, El Malecón begins, a coastal highway and Havana's front porch, geographically 144 kilometres from Miami; ideologically, light years away. Centro's main artery, Calle San Rafael, runs west from Parque Central, the heart of the city. West of the golden dome of Capitolio, lies the curiously engaging Barrio Chino. Here, during the 1950s, Graham Greene's Wormwold was shocked to find 'every permissible vice'. Its seedy side is now concealed behind a gaudy cluster of pseudo-Chinese restaurants. Further west towards Vedado lies Cayo Hueso, named by the cigar workers returning from Key West in the early 20th century. Down at heel, but high on Afro-Cuban spirit, Santería rituals and artistic expression erupt to the frenetic beats of the rumba.

Vedado

The mercurial *municipio* of Vedado is a cultural showcase, hedonist's Mecca and political nerve centre. Laid out in 1859, Vedado was a whizz of colonial planning: a grid of breezy, tree-lined avenues and well-groomed parks, oozing a Zen-like tranquillity. Lured by the promise of an unsullied suburban idyll, La Habana Vieja's bourgeoisie upped sticks and headed out, leaving the poor to stew in the old town.

Vedado's new, elite-seeking denizens soon established the district's identity as the cradle of culture. Galleries, theatres and concert halls brought an artistic energy to languid avenues, lined with sleepy neoclassical mansions. US neocolonial rule and capitalist excess transformed Vedado into a post-modern wasteland of thrusting monoliths, sleek art deco tower blocks and swanky hotels. Meanwhile, the mob worked on its psyche. In cahoots with Batista, the Lansky brothers and Lucky Luciano created a tropical Las Vegas, where the A-list glamorama – Ginger, Frankie and co – were jetted in to fuel the American fantasy, leaving in its wake an entertainment Mecca of X-rated nightspots and grandiose theatres. To the west, Vedado wears a very different face: Plaza de la Revolución, a bleak landscape of government buildings, dominated by the iconic monuments to Che Guevara and José Martí.

Miramar

Beyond Vedado, west of the Río Almendares, lies the US-style garden city of Miramar. It is the closest thing to Havana chi chi, with its refined boulevards dotted with art nouveau mansions and coiffured foliage, influenced by the airs and graces of its early

20th-century upper-class residents. As the Revolution came and capitalist excess went, Miramar was transformed into a ghost town, its privileged classes heading off to clone Miami as their Miramar home from home. Nowadays, its soothing suburban languor appeals to diplomats, expats, businessmen and Cuban nouveaux riches, with new, high-rise glossy hotels rubbing shoulders with embassies, shopping malls and exclusive restaurants. It may lack the verve and stellar attractions of other *municipios*, but it has some of the best *paladares* and nightlife in Havana.

Around Havana

As the 20th century was ushered in, Havana spread its wings. Opulent villas and exclusive seaside clubs sprouted westward, reaching as far as Siboney and Cubanacán in Playa. With the lofty artistic ideals of the 1960s a national school of art was unveiled in Cubanacán, but the ambitious project never crystallized, and the innovative work of three eminent architects now lies neglected.

Further west, Marina Hemingway, polished and manufactured, lures seafaring tourists with the promise of all manner of marine endeavour. Eastern development was minimal until the French constructed a 550-m tunnel in 1958 under the mouth of the harbour. From here a highway skirts the coast, cutting through a dour glut of Soviet-style apartment blocks, decaying under the onslaught of salty winds and tropical heat. Hemingway aficionados flock to Cojímar, the seaside village that featured in *The Old Man and the Sea*, now a modern concrete jungle. Regla and Guanabacoa have maintained their small town identity more successfully. Steeped in Santería, they are a potent immersion into the Afro-Cuban reality without the tourist spin.

Sun worshippers play with the locals, or just bask and bronze on the palm-studded beaches of Playas del Este, the nearest beaches to Havana. To the south of the city, you can tour the Botanical Gardens and Parque Lenín, indulging in outdoor pursuits such as horse riding, boating or swimming to blow away the city fumes.

Trip planner

Havana burns year round but the cooler times are December to March, when the breeze is that bit stronger and the atmosphere is less humid. The cheapest times tend to be in hurricane season, the riskiest months being September to November, although you can still get lots of sunshine and hurricanes don't come every year. The best times for the top festivals divide neatly into two: July- August for carnival and dance festivals, and December-January for film, jazz and dance festivals, New Year, and regattas.

Two-four days

Several days will give you time to get under the skin of the colonial heart, La Habana Vieja, and explore the modern attractions of Vedado. You can tour iconic hotels, trawl Hemingway haunts and mobster hangouts, and visit top sights. By night, dine in one of Havana's quirky eateries, from colonial mansions to humble apartments or movie sets, and revel *habanero* style in a potent cocktail of rum, pumping rumba and impassioned salsa. Dedicate the lion's share of daytime activity to La Habana Vieja. Soak up the belle époque architecture and the city's cast of characters on the Plaza de Armas. Head north to the Columbus Cathedral or stroll south to the faded glory of La Plaza Vieja, before heading west to the imposing dome of Capitolio. Escape the afternoon heat and explore the old town's main artery, Calle Obispo. Wander into its back streets, watch some of Cuba's famed artists at work, and stock pile Cuban music CDs, cigars and *Havana Club*. Inject some more rum and revelry, with live salsa and punchy cocktails at Obispo's lively bars. Then take your pick of the museums. Art lovers shouldn't miss the Cuban section of the Museo Nacional Palacio de Bellas Artes. For the full revolutionary low down, head to the Museo de la Revolución. Less time is needed for the Partagás cigar tour, or develop a finer appreciation of the national drink at the rum museum.

★ Ten of the best

Best

1 El Malecón Wander along Havana's mystical oceanfront esplanade at sunset.

2 Callejón Hamel A great free Sunday entertainment feast of pumping rumba, Santería divinations and artistic spirit, p68.

3 El Delirio Habanero Great music, upbeat atmosphere and fantastic setting overlooking Plaza de la Revolución, p157.

4 Museo de la Revolución The story of Cuba's political history in mind-blowing detail. A revolutionary kitsch fest, p59.

5 Hotel Nacional Cruise up the Beverly Hills-style driveway, sashay through the sumptuous lobby, order a cocktail on the terrace, and soak up one of the best views of the city, p140.

6 Museo Nacional de Bellas Artes Cuba's premier museum, a US$500 million showcase of Cuban and international art, p60. If you are short on time, head straight to floor three for the museum's highlight, the Cuban Modern Art collection.

7 Cementerio Colón Havana's city of the dead; an extravaganza of funereal sculpture, steeped in mysticism and historical significance, p74.

8 Casa de la Música A top venue for Cuba's big name bands, regulars include *Los Van Van* and *NG La Banda*. For a more local feel, check out the raunchy Sunday afternoon matinées, p160.

9 Paladar dining Hearty Cuban staples, or inventive international fare, at home with the family, p123.

10 Playas del Este Just a half-hour-taxi ride away, a sun worshipper's beach Babylon, p93.

Allow a day to stroll Vedado's boulevards, and take in the ethereal atmosphere of Cementerio Colón, and more doses of revolutionary iconography on the Plaza de La Revolución. For sweeter pleasures, engage with the locals as they wait to indulge in ice cream at Coppelia - used in the movie *Fresa y Chocolate*. For a taste of the fabulous fifties, wander up to the *Hotel Nacional* and out onto the terrace for one of the best cocktails with a view. For a less soft focus perspective on the city, amble the streets of Centro and on Sundays don't miss the *Peña Cultural* in Callejón Hamel.

Kick start the evening line-up with a daiquiri at the *Inglaterra*'s pavement café, *El Louvre*, and absorb the hullabaloo of Parque Central. Stroll the mystical Malecón as the sun goes down. Dine with the family at one of Vedado's top paladares, then, late evening, head to the National Theatre for the refined musical extravaganza of *El Delirio Habanero*. Follow it up with super-charged salsa at *Café Cantante Mi Habana* nightclub. For international dining, head out to Miramar. Relax in the elegant courtyard of *La Cocina de Liliam*, and enjoy home cooking, before moving up a tempo at one of the top venues, *Casa de la Música; El Tropical*, for more raunchy salsa, or the *Tropicana,* the mother of all cabarets.

A week or more

If you have the time to venture further afield. Just a half-hour taxi ride from Parque Central, you can laze on Caribbean beaches, breeze through parks and gardens or soak up the frenzy of a baseball match. To experience rural Cuba, you can easily slot in a well-organized overnight excursion at a tourist office, but it is no trouble to hop on a bus and do it independently. Viñales is a rural idyll in the heart of the best tobacco growing area, with mogotes – steep-sided limestone mountains – providing a Chinese flavour to the landscape. Overnighting in Trinidad is not to be missed. About five-hour bus ride away, you travel through fields of sugar and cattle up into the Sierra de Guamuhaya and along the south coast to reach this most precious of colonial towns.

Contemporary Havana

The world according to Fidel has never been an easy place to get your head around. The 21st-century Cuba brand of tropical Marxism remains as ambivalent as it is alluring: a Caribbean party island where the cheap rum flows and the cigars are the finest in the world; the last word in revolutionary chic; and the source of global pan-Latin musical delirium. It doesn't take long to clock that this is not your standard Caribbean exoticism. The fantasy of millennial joie de vivre is soon stripped away by the reality of economic hardship, social paranoia and intellectual stagnation.

Arriving in Havana you could not be blamed for thinking that you had stepped into the twilight zone. When Cuba's communist sidekicks collapsed like dominoes in the 1990s, Fidel's dreams of Marxist utopia turned to ashes. The so-called Special Period transformed the city from a place with one of the highest standards of living in Latin America into a medieval landscape, and the regime's ideological foundations – cradle-to-grave education, housing and health care for all, began to crumble along with Havana's colonial treasures. As the lights went out over Havana, the neon of Miami became ever more inviting. Discontent soared, the regime tightened its ideological strait-jacket, and Havana became a city on the verge of a nervous breakdown.

El Comandante, now in his mid-70s, is a withered image of the iconic revolutionary zealot who claimed even before the Revolution "History will absolve me". Derided as a despot by many, worshipped as a Saviour by others, Fidel remains an enigma. In a totalitarian country where media spin takes on a whole new meaning, Fidel watching has become a national pastime. For Cubans, who see their destiny wrapped up in the epic David and Goliath struggle against the imperial enemy, the Revolution is a symbol of national identity. Over rum and dominoes, superstitious *habaneros* ponder the symbolism of his every move in an attempt to interpret the health of the nation. Despite rumours of

Alzheimer's and cancer, many of skewed Miami origin, Fidel continues to transfix with his Olympic orations. For the *Día de Los Trabajadores* 2002, from the Plaza de la Revolución, Fidel delivered his customary verbal assault on the evil empire of Uncle Sam to the flag-waving rapture of the masses. *Campesinos*, drafted in for the day, chanted on cue to Fidel's sabre-toothed attack against the unjust treatment of five Cubans imprisoned in the USA on charges of spying.

Since 11 September, the US-Cuban plot has thickened. Faced with the hawkish posture of the Bush administration towards the "axis of evil", Castro symbolically cast off his military fatigues to receive one of America's whitest doves, former president Jimmy Carter. On 16 May 2002, Carter delivered perhaps the most open discourse on civil rights on Cuban soil to date, broadcast live and uncensored from the University of Havana. Fidel's motivations are as ambiguous as ever. A placatory gesture? Or an attempt to convey that the Cuban dream is still alive and kicking?

A hard line American foreign policy seems set to dominate the Cuban agenda for some considerable time, compounding the daily anguish of *habaneros* on the bread line, struggling under the weight of a crippling embargo. For George W Bush, politically driven by the power of the Miami-Cuban vote, softening the approach on Cuba would amount to political suicide. However, as the Elián González debate revealed, public attitudes Stateside appear to be taking a more moderate line, indicative in the House of Representatives' vote to lift sanctions on US travel to Cuba.

While Castro blames Havana's woes on the capitalist arch enemy, his very downfall could come from within. Project Varela, the initiative of *habanero* electrician Oswaldo Paya, is an unprecedented campaign for civil rights based upon a series of demands, including freedom of speech, liberation of political prisoners and free elections.

If the petition is supported by 10,000 signatures, the motion, according to the Cuban constitution, must be put to a referendum.

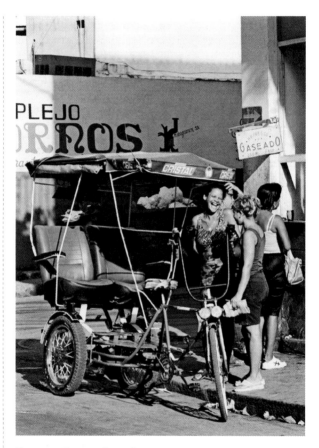

Conversation on the calle

Habaneros hitch a ride on a bicitaxi, one of Havana's myriad transport options, and catch up on la bola (the gossip).

It's a bitter irony that the due to the government's media strangle-hold *habaneros* are largely unaware of the campaign's very existence.

The dawn of mass tourism has opened a Pandora's box. When Havana was designated a World Heritage Site in 1982, Fidel had an epiphany. The city he had neglected for decades was an Aladdin's cave of architectural marvels and tropical pleasures. Through a series of joint ventures with European and Canadian partners, many of Havana's ailing façades have been given a facelift, and the city's colonial heart is gradually being restored to its former belle époque splendour. Ominously, Havana seems in danger of overdosing on its own tourist cachet. Mammoth rehabilitation projects threaten to morph Havana's architectural eclecticism into a homogenous mass of regulation creamy façades, polished iron-works and manicured squares, where you don't step on the grass.

In 1994, Fidel was forced to trade with the enemy, replacing the patronage of the Soviet block for the most potent symbol of the evil empire. The dollar was legalized and the tourist bandwagon slipped into gear. The greenback, reviled and revered in equal measure, became a last ditch attempt to pull Cuba out of economic and social collapse. With the dangling carrot of private enterprise, Cubans were permitted to open up their homes as restaurants, and offer private accommodation to paying guests, only later to be hammered by astronomical taxes and threats of fines for non-compliance by a bureaucratic minefield. Embracing their new quasi-entrepreneurial status, Cubans have introduced much-needed gastro-twists into Cuba's starchy fodder, and more B&B creature comforts into the tourist accommodation package. While Fidel's lofty revolutionary promises aimed to rid the city of its seedy role as America's backyard brothel, he has instead created a sin bin for a new breed of traveller who comes to soak up the allure of the 'fabulous fifties' or check it all out before 'he' goes. In a city where the average monthly wage is US$10, and a tourist shells out US$6 for a cocktail, it's not surprising that the social fabric is unravelling. The oldest professions in the book are enjoying a vocational vogue, with hustling and prostitution satisfying a specialized traveller market. Many of Cuba's highly skilled elite are giving up their jobs to drive cabs and moonlight cleaning hotel rooms. Young *habaneros* learn how to talk a good game to big tipping travellers, as a buck here and a buck there soon amounts to more than a heart surgeon earns in a year. With the peso value decimated, *habanero* survival depends on infiltrating the dollar economy, by fair means or foul.

Police are now part of Havana's daily landscape, stationed on every block, assuring this tourist gravy train doesn't go off the rails, safeguarding the greenback rollout in a tropical apartheid. Fidel's plain-clothed thought police, the Communist Defence League, remain the eyes and ears of the regime, ready to snitch on any liberal anti-*fidelista* tendencies. *La Lucha* (the struggle) is the tragi-comic Cuban response to a life of subsistence living, infected with paranoia and fear. Waiting is something *habaneros* excel at: waiting for buses that never come, waiting to see if tourism will bring Cuba the benefits it is promised, waiting to see what will happen when, or if, Fidel goes.

This Cuban reality is certainly far removed from its mass-produced global image. Tourists consume the Hollywood-style pulp fiction: a heady tale of an evil empire, starring gun-toting revolutionaries and hedonistic literary giants, played out to an electrifying soundtrack, set against a seductive Caribbean backdrop. Meanwhile the Cuban psyche embarks on a road less travelled.

There are direct and non-direct scheduled flights to the José Martí international airport at Havana, 18 km from La Habana Vieja. There are also scheduled and charter flights to Varadero International, some 144 km and three hours from Havana.

Havana is very spread out. La Habana Vieja to Miramar along the Malecón (the seafront boulevard) is over 8 km. Buses can be tricky for the uninitiated, involving complicated queuing procedures and a lot of pushing and shoving. A more leisurely way of getting around is to hire a *bicitaxi* (bicycle taxi).

Getting there

Air

From UK and the rest of Europe Direct flights are available from Amsterdam, Frankfurt, London, Madrid, Milan, Munich, Paris, Rome and Shannon. Air Jamaica flies from London, while Air France and Iberia operate connecting services. Direct flights are approximately nine hours. The high seasons cover the Easter period, the July-August European summer and the last two-three weeks of December. Prices quoted here include all taxes apart from the Cuban departure tax.

   Air Jamaica's low season prices vary from £431-515 from London. Its high season prices range from £574-641. **Iberia**, via Madrid, has flights from £463-517 (low season) up to £594 in the high season. **Air France**, from London via Paris, low season quotes are £473-517. High season prices rise to £595-640. Paris -Havana in low-high season costs for £409-565. **Air Europa** offers two-month tickets from Madrid for £507-575, while *Iberia* fares from Madrid are £548-560, valid for three months. **Martinair** from London via Amsterdam offers flights in the low season from £455 up to £654 in the high season. All these flights arrive in Havana around 2000-2130. The state airline, **Cubana de Aviación**, is sometimes cheaper, but not recommended. Packages including hotels and ground arrangements can work out cheaper. Early booking is essential as agents need at least 14 days' notice to get confirmations from Havana.

From North America Since 1962, US citizens have only been permitted to visit Cuba providing they can prove they are travelling for journalistic, cultural, sporting or scientific purposes. However, despite the risk of hefty fines, US travellers are increasingly travelling via a gateway city, such as Nassau, Mexico City, Cancún, Montego Bay, Kingston or Grand Cayman. On 23 July 2002, the House of Representatives voted by a 240-186 majority to

Airlines and travel agent websites

Aerocaribe, www.aerocaribe.com
Air Canada, www.aircanada.ca, T 18882472262 (Canada)
Air Europa, www.aireuropa.com, T 0870 2401501 (UK),
T 0034 971 178 100 (Spain)
Air France, www.airfrance.com, T 0845 0845111 (UK),
T 0033 820820820.
Air Jamaica, www.airjamaica.com, T020 8570 7999 (UK),
T 1-800-5235585 in the USA and the Caribbean.
Captivating Cuba, www.captivating-cuba.co.uk,
T 0870 8870123 (UK)
Condor, www.condor.de, T 01802337135 (Germany)
Conference World Tours, www.conferencetours.com,
T 416 221 6411 (Canada)
Cubalinda, www.cubalinda.com, T 0053 7553980 (Cuba)
Cubana, www.cubana.cu
Cuban Adventures, www.cubanadventures.com,
T 18772822386 (USA/Canada)
Havanatur, www.havanatur.cu, T 01707 646463 (UK)
Iberia, www.iberia.com, T 0845 6012854 (UK),
T 0034 902 400500 (Spain)
Interchange, www.interchange.uk.com, T 020 8760 0031 (UK)
Journey Latin America, www.journeylatinamerica.co.uk
T 020 8747 3108 (UK)
Martinair, www.martinair.com, T 0031 206011767 (Netherlands)
Mexicana, www.mexicana.com, T 020 8492 0000 (UK),
T 8005317921 (USA/Canada)
MILA Tours, www.MILAtours.com, T 18003677378 (USA)
South American Experience,
www.southamericanexperience.co.uk, T 020 7976 5511 (UK)
STA, www.statravel.co.uk, www.sta-travel.com,
T 0870 1600599 (UK)

★ **Ways to live on the peso**

Best

- Baseball game, p189.
- Chinese food market, p65.
- Pekin vegetarian restaurant, p141.
- Paladar El Helecho, p135.
- Vintage car boulevard cruising.

ease restrictions on travel and trade with Cuba. At the time of writing it had not gone before the senate. *Cubana* offers good deals from neighbouring gateways: US$180 round trip from Cancún (US$279 *Mexicana de Aviación/Aerocaribe*), US$189 from Nassau, US$219 from Freeport, Bahamas, US$333 from Santo Domingo and US$225 from Grand Cayman. *Air Jamaica*'s fares from Montego Bay or Kingston are considerably more. From Canada there are direct flights from Montréal and Toronto with high, low and shoulder seasons, the cheapest from Montréal being around US$790 in September. See also Directory, p201, for further information.

Airport information Terminal 3 is for international flights. It has exchange facilities open during banking hours, snack bars, shops, car rental and a 24-hour tourist information bureau (**Infotur**, T 666101) with limited information. The terminal is safe at night. Immigration formalities are often time consuming. Taxis line up outside arrivals and fares range from US$15-20, but US$18 is commonly asked to La Habana Vieja, 18 km away. There is no public bus service to the international terminal. *Víazul* operates a transfer service from some hotels from Vedado for US$4. There is no airport hotel. The seating at the airport is uncomfortable and the food in the departure lounge is awful.
Airport departure tax is US$20.

Travel extras

Customs You can take out tobacco worth US$2,000 with a receipt, or 50 cigars without a receipt, up to six bottles of rum and personal jewellery. To take out works of art you need permission from the Registro Nacional de Bienes Culturales de la Dirección de Patrimonio del Ministerio de Cultura. Vendors can also help, see p182. It is prohibited to bring in fresh fruit and vegetables.

Entry Visitors from most countries need a passport, return ticket and 30-day tourist card. Tourist cards can be obtained from Cuban embassies, airlines or approved travel agents, US$15-35. If you do not have a pre-booked hotel voucher you may be asked to pay for three nights minimum in a hotel on arrival. However, as long as immigration see the name of a hotel (for example, Hotel Plaza) on your tourist card they are unlikely to enquire further. US travellers should contact the **Cuban Interests Section**, a Cuban Government office, at 2630 16th St NW, Washington DC 20009, T 202-7978518. (Information also from www.cubalinda.com.)

Money The monetary unit is the *peso Cubano*. The official exchange rate is US$1=1 peso, but the free rate fluctuates between 25-30 pesos = US$1. There is also a *peso convertible* on a par with the US dollar, with different notes and coins. It is fully exchangeable with the US dollar and the Euro, but worthless outside Cuba. Food in the markets (*agromercados*) and at street stalls can be bought in pesos, but only change small amounts at a time. This can be done in *Cadecas* (exchange houses) or on the street. Tourist establishments will only accept US dollars, or in some cases, Euro. Travellers' cheques issued on US bank paper and credit cards issued in the USA are not accepted. American Express, no matter where issued, is unacceptable. It is best to bring plenty of cash. There is usually a US$ minimum withdrawal from a smattering of ATMs. It may be quicker and easier to queue at a bank to get a dollar cash advance on your credit card than to trail around looking for a working ATM. There are no toll-free numbers for you to call if your credit card is lost or stolen. You will have to phone home to the financial institution which issued you the card in order to put a stop on its use. Make a note of this number before you leave home, together with your credit card account number, and keep them separate from your card. See also *Asistur*, p205.

Safety Havana is generally safe, but street lighting is poor so care is needed when walking at night. There is a lot of good-natured hassling on the street. Foreigners will be offered almost anything. Despite government crackdowns and increased penalties, prostitution is widespread. The age of consent is 18. Foreigners seeking sex are seen as fair game. Hotels are not allowed to let Cubans enter in the company of foreigners. Sexual encounters now often take place in *casas particulares*, where there is little security and lots of risk. Cubans who sell their services (sexual or otherwise) are known as *jineteros* (jockeys), because they 'ride on the back' of the tourists.

Telephone At the time of going to press (Autumn 2002) all telephone numbers were accurate. However, there are ongoing changes to the prefixes of all Cuban numbers. For further information while in Havana dial Etecsa number 66 6111.

Vaccinations There is no malaria in Cuba but there are periodic outbreaks of dengue fever so take insect repellent. Bring in all the medicines you might need as they are difficult to find. Also bring your own contraceptives, tampons, sun cream, and photographic supplies.

Getting around

Bus

There are huge double buses pulled by an articulated truck, called *camellos* (camels) because of their shape. They are hot, sweaty and uncomfortably crowded at all times. Entrance is at the middle double doors, 20 centavos. *Camellos* cover the main suburbs: M1 (pink) Calle G, Vedado, via Carlos III and El Floridita to Alamar; M2 (blue) Parque El Curita, esquina Reina y Avenida Italia (Galiano), via Plaza de la Revolución, Boyeros and airport terminals 1 and 2 to Santiago de las Vegas; M3 (yellow) Ciudad Deportiva, via Lawton, Guanabacoa to Zone 8 in Alamar; M6 (brown) Calle 21, Vedado, via Malecón and La Víbora to Reparto Eléctrico (near Parque Lenín). Ask for the right queue. Discover who is last (la última) for the bus you want as people mark their places and then wander off until the bus comes. Regular buses (blue) cost 40 centavos. The 222 and 264 buses run from Egido near the train terminal to Miramar and Playa, via Vedado. P1 and P2 both originate in San Miguel del Padrón and run every 20 minutes: P1 through Luyanó, Infanta, Vedado and along Línea; P2 through Lawton, La Víbora, Ciudad Deportiva, Víazul bus terminal, Vedado 26 y 41 to Miramar.

There are two **long distance bus companies** for dollar-paying tourists: Astro and Víazul. Astro is the state-run bus company which has a few seats for tourists on each of its buses. Its base is central and convenient for many hotels or private accommodation. Víazul is a tourist operation and is more expensive but more comfortable, punctual and efficient, with a/c (take fleece at night). It is a convenient way of visiting Trinidad, Viñales and other excursions. **Astro**, Terminal de Omnibus Nacional, Boyeros y 19 de Mayo (third left via 19 de Mayo entrance), T 8703397, is near the Plaza de la Revolución, Vedado. **Víazul**, Avenida 26 entre Avenida Zoológico y Ulloa, Nuevo Vedado, T 8811413, www.viazul.cu Online reservations are possible with your credit card debited in Canadian dollars. A taxi from here is around US$5-7 to La Habana Vieja or Centro.

Car

Car hire is not recommended in Havana; roads are badly signed and there have been many accidents. Out of the city, however, roads are fairly empty. Drive on the right. Car hire agencies can be found at the airport or in the reception area of hotels, see Directory, p201. Minimum US$40 a day (US$50 a/c) with limited mileage of 100 km a day, and US$8-20 a day optional insurance, or US$50-88 per day unlimited mileage; cheaper rates over seven days. Credit cards are accepted, or cash or travellers' cheques paid in advance; you must also present your passport and home driving licence. Always carry the rental agreement and your driving licence with you, otherwise you will face an on the spot fine.

Petrol costs US$0.75 for regular and US$0.90 for *especial* per litre and must be paid for in US dollars. **Cupet-Cimex** (green logo) and **Oro Negro** are open 24 hrs. Unofficial 'supervisors' monitor car parking spaces for US$0.50.

Cycling

Cycling is a good way to see Havana, especially the suburbs, or for day trips to the beach at Playas del Este. An absolute must is cruising the cycle lane the length of the Malecón. Take care at night as there are few street lights and bikes are not fitted with lamps. Cycle lanes are marked by concrete bumps, colloquially called *mojones* (cow pats), or standard broken yellow lines. A white bicycle in a blue circle with an arrow indicates the cycle lane and mandatory routes for bikes.

Bicycle parking lots, *parqueo de bicicleta*, 1 peso, open until 1800. Always lock your bike and remove all accessories. Poncheros are small private businesses that crudely fix punctures. The Ciclobus, 20 centavos, is a bus with the seats removed and special ramps at the rear of the bus for loading, designed to take cyclists through the tunnel under the harbour to the Vía Blanca dual carriageway and Playas del Este. You are not permitted to cycle through this tunnel. Queue at Parque El Curita on Dragones, one block west of Fraternidad.

Ferry

There are ferries from La Habana Vieja to Casablanca and Regla, which depart from San Pedro opposite Calle Santa Clara. If you are facing the water, the Casablanca ferry docks on the left side of the pier and goes out in a left curve towards that headland, and the Regla ferry docks on the right side and goes out in a right curve.

Taxi

Dollar tourist taxis charge for the distance, not for waiting time. On short routes, fares are metered. See Directory, p201, for companies. For longer trips some companies charge by the hour or per kilometre. *Colectivos* are large old American gas guzzlers operating on fixed routes and pick you up only if you know where to stand for certain destinations. Travelling on them is an adventure and a complicated cultural experience. Tell the driver where to drop you. Fixed 10 pesos Cubanos fare. If you are travelling from La Habana Vieja to Vedado, the best spot to wait is next to Prado y Neptuno restaurant opposite the Hotel Telégrafo on Parque Central. Flag one down, yell "veinte-tres" (Calle 23). A nod is your cue to get in. Have your 10 pesos ready to hand over when you want to exit. As foreigners shouldn't really be picked up, avoid brandishing too much tourist paraphernalia.

Particulares are private taxis. A *particular* who pays his tax will usually display a red sticker '*Pasaje*' on the windscreen. Some have meters, but if not, 10 km should cost around US$5. For long distances the price should be around US$10-15 per hour depending on your negotiating skills. Beware of moonlighters without the licence sticker; you have no come-back in the case of mishaps. Cubans are not allowed to carry foreigners in their vehicles, but they do. *Bicitaxis* (bicycle or tricycle taxis) are a pleasant way to travel. La Habana Vieja to Vedado US$3, or pay around US$5 per hour, bargaining is acceptable. The *cocomóvil* is bright yellow and shaped like a coconut shell on a 125 cc motor bike, 2 passengers, no safety belts, agree the US$ fare before the journey, typically

US$3 from the *Hotel Nacional* to La Habana Vieja. Less conspicuous are the *Rentar una fantasía* vehicles, using the same 125 cc engine but the vehicle is designed as an antique motor car. For the real thing, *Gran Car*, T 8335647, rents classic cars (including Oldsmobiles, Mercury '54, Buicks and Chevvy '55) with driver, maximum 4 passengers, US$15 per hour or US$18 per hour for cars without roofs.

Walking
The sights of La Habana Vieja are best explored on foot. Watch out for potholes. Vedado is very spread out and Miramar even more so, so be prepared for covering many miles. Strolling from Parque Central down the Prado, then along the Malecón to the Hotel Nacional will take around 45 minutes. From La Rampa to Cementerio Colón is a good half-an-hour walk.

Tours and tourist information

Tours
The easiest way of getting around the city of Havana is with *Vaivén*, T 669713/ 249626-28, run by *Rumbos*. For US$4 per day you can get on and off a 30-seater bus along a route with 23 stops; buses pass every 50 minutes between 0900-2140. From Calle Monserrate, outside the *Floridita* bar, the bus goes to Castillo del Morro, the Malecón, Avenida 5 and Avenida 1 in Miramar, the Palacio de las Convenciones and the tourist complex at La Giraldilla, returning via the Plaza de la Revolución and the university before returning to the Malecón, along the Prado to the Capitolio and back to Calle Monserrate. There is a guide on board if you need information.

State-owned travel agencies have bureaux in all the major hotels. For tour options, see box. Guides speak Spanish, English, French, Italian or German; the tours are well-organized and good value, but actual departure depends on a minimum number of passengers (usually six).

→ Tours in and around Havana

Tours can be arranged of colonial and modern Havana by bus. Examples include a tour of the city's colonial sites (US$15, 4 hours); a trip to the *Tropicana* cabaret (US$60, 4 hours, US$70 with supper).

Further afield Guamá and the Península de Zapata with tour of a crocodile farm (US$44, 9 hours); Viñales and Pinar del Río, visiting *mogotes* (steep-sided limestone mountains), caves and a tobacco factory (US$44, 9 hours); a day on the beach at Varadero (US$35 or US$45 with lunch, 10 hours, changing room with shower and towel); Colonial Trinidad and Cienfuegos overnight, visiting the exceptionally well-preserved colonial city and the Valle de los Ingenios (US$115); ecological tour of Las Terrazas with walking and river bathing (US$44, 10 hours).

Tourist information

Tourist information offices **Infotur**, www.infotur.cu, is supposed to have maps, guides, postcards, phonecards, film, CDs, cassettes, magazines, photocopying and fax, but some are just kiosks without all the facilities. In La Habana Vieja, T 333333, at Obispo entre Habana y Compostela, Obispo y San Ignacio, Obispo y Bernaza and the Terminal de Cruceros. In Playa at Av 5 y 112, T/F 2047036.

Maps

Maps published by **Ediciones GEO** are the best, accurate and up to date. **Instituto Hidrográfico**, Mercaderes entre Obispo y Oficios in La Habana Vieja, T 613625, F 332869, sells maps and charts, both national and regional.

La Habana Vieja 33
The heart of Havana stuffed with the glories of a bygone era and a modern-day tourist Mecca, see opposite page.

Centro 56
The beleagured centre of Havana and the cultural melting pot.

Vedado 70
Former home of the revolutionary headquarters turned bourgeois and bacchanal haven.

Miramar 86
Wealthy suburb with top paladares and nightlife venues found amid art nouveau mansions.

La Habana Vieja

Calle Obispo, chaotic and jam-packed with shops, bars, paladares, galleries and peso food stalls, is La Habana Vieja's main artery. An endless tide of tourists and locals ebbs and flows into vibrant alleys before spilling out onto the *Plaza de Armas*, the old town's social hub. To the northwest lies one of Cuba's most romantic and architecturally harmonious squares, *Plaza de la Catedral*, with the *Columbus Cathedral*, the finest example of Cuban baroque.

Follow the *Hemingway trail* to the west, where grey-bearded men sip US$6 mojitos at La Bodeguita del Medio, the shrine to Big Ern, and then set off on a pleasure pilgrimage to Havana's murkier side. On the south-eastern corner of Plaza de Armas, newly spruced *Calle Oficios* leads to the *Iglesia San Francisco de Asís*, surrounded by a clutch of lively bars, museums and hotels.

Streets, steeped in superstition, wind south from here, where the habanero *youth sport the bracelets of Santería, rather than the latest designer logos; religious effigies hang from the doorways and, hidden within,* babalawos *(priests) vibrate in frenzied rhythm, as they perform the rituals of Santería.*

Southern La Habana Vieja, shabby, hard-pressed and frenetic, is not for the fainthearted. Life spews out from behind the crumbling façades of cramped residences, and the brutal spasms of La Lucha *are laid bare. Few tourists make it to the serene* **Residencia Santa Clara** *or the* **Museo Casa Natal de José Martí,** *and even fewer experience the area's compelling street life. Men hunch over domino tables and kids play baseball, oblivious to the mountains of rubble and hazardous coils of electrical wires. Old women discuss 'El Jefe' in the queues for their rations at the local* bodegas, *and gossip and heckle from across the balconies, where makeshift antennae transmit the latest* telenovelas *from foreign parts.*

▸ *See Sleeping, p101, Eating and drinking, p123, and Bars and clubs, p145 and p153.*

◉ Sights

★ Plaza de Armas
Map 6, D5, p256

Plaza de Armas is La Habana Vieja's oldest and most vibrant square. Despite the bands of Hemingway clones, ambling in a mojito haze with *jineteros* in hot pursuit, the central park with graceful palms, pink floral smatterings and marble benches is one of the most serene spots in the city. At the centre of the park stands the elegant statue of revolutionary landowner Carlos Manuel de Céspedes, the 'Father of the Nation', who initiated the ten-year war against Spanish colonial rule in 1868. Once the political nucleus of Havana, the park is framed by corpulent colonial architecture and ringed by second-hand bookstalls.

El Templete
Plaza de Armas entre Obispo y O'Reilly. *Map 6, D5, p256*

In the northeast corner of the Plaza de Armas is the church of El Templete. Built in 1828, it was the first neoclassical building in Havana. A column erected in front in 1754 marks the spot where the first mass, and town council was celebrated under a *ceiba* tree in 1519. The event is celebrated by *habaneros* every 16 November. Legend has it that a sapling of the same *ceiba* tree, blown down by a hurricane in 1753, was planted on the same spot, and under its branches the supposed bones of Columbus reposed in state before being taken to the cathedral. This tree was cut down in 1828, the present tree planted, and the Doric temple opened. The temple houses allegorical canvases by the renowned French painter Jean Bautiste Vermay, and first director of the Academia Nacional de Bellas Artes. Vermay's ashes are contained in the urn, alongside a bust of the painter, that forms the room's centrepiece.

Castillo de la Real Fuerza and Museo de la Cerámica Cubana

O'Reilly entre Av de Puerto y Tacón, **T** 8615010, museum,
T 8616130. *0800-1900. US$2. Museum: Mon-Sat 0830-1645.
US$1, free under 15yrs.* Map 6, C5, p256

Considering the primitive resources available when it was built,
this muscular colonial fort is an architectural marvel. With walls
6 m thick and 10 m high, huge triangular bulwarks at each corner,
and a drawbridge leading over the moat to the vaulted interior, it
is Cuba's oldest building and the second oldest fort in the New
World. It was built in 1558 to protect the city's lucrative harbour
from the likes of pirate Jacques de Sores, who razed Havana to the
ground in 1555. An architectural quantum leap it may have been,
impenetrable it wasn't, failing to deter further onslaughts by the
English in 1622, 1623 and 1638. Perched atop the picturesque
tower is the rather limp bronze weathervane of La Giraldilla.
Symbol of Havana, it represents Doña Isabel de Bobadilla who
waited in vain for her husband Governor Hernando de Soto to
return from his lofty attempts to conquer Florida. Her love-struck
image graces the *Havana Club* label. Inside the castle is an armour
museum with Cuban ceramic art dating from the 1940s onwards.

Museo de la Ciudad (Palacio de los Capitanes Generales)

Plaza de Armas entre Obispo y O'Reilly, **T** 8615779. *Daily
0900-1930. US$3, guided visit US$4, admission includes entry to Casa
de la Plata. A combined city and museum tour US$8, charge for
photos US$2, video US$10. There are no explanations, even in
Spanish.* Map 6, C4, p256

On the west side of Plaza de Armas stands the city's historical
museum. Built in 1780 as the Palace of the Captains General, it is a
charming example of Cuban baroque architecture. Spanish
governors and the presidents lived here until 1917, when it

became City Hall. It houses a large collection of 19th-century furnishings. There are portraits of patriots, military memorabilia and a grandly laid out dining room. The lavish throne room, plushly upholstered in deep-red satin, was intended for the King of Spain but never used; no Spanish king or queen ever came to Cuba in colonial times. The building was the site of the signing of the 1898 treaty between Spain and the USA. The elegant inner courtyard contains Royal Palms, the Cuban national tree, and is often the setting for *quinceañeras* photo sessions, as 15-year-old girls, like prom queens, celebrate their coming of age. An extension to the museum is the Casa de la Plata, entre Mercaderes y Oficios, which exhibits fine pieces, jewellery and old frescoes.

Palacio del Segundo Cabo (Instituto Cubano del Libro)
Plaza de Armas. *Map 6, C5, p256*

The Palacio del Segundo Cabo, a baroque construction that sits on the north side of the plaza, was completed in 1772 and housed the Royal Post Office and then the Supreme Court of Justice before finding a stately vocation as the private residence of the Captains General. The inner courtyard, with spiralling vines and intricate balconies, is a fine example of the Moorish influence on Spanish architecture. It now houses the Instituto Cubano del Libro, responsible for the promotion of literature and a couple of bookshops.

Museo Nacional de Historia Natural
Plaza de Armas, Obispo 61, **T** 8632687, museo@mnhnc.inf.cu
Tue-Fri 0930-1730, Sat and Sun 0930-1630. US$3.
Written information is in Spanish only.   *Map 6, D5, p256*

The natural history museum is the most visited in the city, thanks to the large numbers of schoolchildren who enjoy the child-friendly exhibitions. There's no shortage of stuffed animals, and other endemic species, displays on the evolution of life, and

Colonial crème de la crème

From sleek art deco to the whimsical baroque, Havana is an architectural treasure trove.

exhibits of Cuban-Indian archaeology. Budding young Patrick Moores should head for the planetarium. Also worth a look are the reproduction cave paintings of Punta del Este, Isla de la Juventud. To complete the theme, the museum hosts expo-ventas on the ground floor with paintings and plastic arts relating to natural history. The museum appears to be waiting in vain for an estimated US$2 million from the government to expand.

★ La Catedral de San Cristóbal de La Habana
Plaza de la Catedral. *Mon-Sat 0930-1230, Sun 0830-1230, mass at 1030. Map 6, B4, p256*

Plaza de la Catedral is Havana's most romantic and architecturally harmonious square. When the Spanish rolled in, this waterlogged terrain was known as the Plazuela de la Ciénaga (swamp square) before becoming the site of the first Spanish aqueduct in Latin America. In 1748 Jesuit missionaries began construction of a church on the site. When the order was expelled in 1767 by Carlos III, it was converted into a cathedral and the square renamed.

The sublime Havana Cathedral was completed in 1777 and dominates the northern end of the square. It is surrounded by elegant 18th-century baroque palaces, with ice-blue wooden shutters and balconies.

Officially dedicated to the Virgin of the Immaculate Conception, it is the most notable baroque building in Havana. Described as "music set in stone" by the author Alejo Carpentier, see p222, it features an eccentric, undulating façade, asymmetrical towers and wooden-ribbed vaulting over its three naves.

! Often referred to as the Columbus cathedral, the bones of Christopher Columbus were allegedly sent here when Santo Domingo was ceded by Spain to France in 1795; they now lie in Santo Domingo (Dominican Republic).

Museo de Arte Colonial

Plaza de la Catedral (in the former Palacio de los Condes de Casa Bayona), **T** 8626440. *Daily 0900-1900. US$2, guide US$1, photos US$2. Map 6, C3, p256*

The unabashed opulence of the 17th-century colonial aristocracy is portrayed through a collection of colonial furniture, wrought ironwork, silverware and porcelain. One room is dedicated to stunning stained-glass *vitrales* and *mediopuntos*, huge stained-glass windows partitioned with lead rather than wood.

Centro de Arte Contemporáneo Wilfredo Lam

San Ignacio 22 esquina Empedrado, just next to the cathedral, **T** 8613419. *Daily 0900-1700. Free. Map 6, B3, p256*

A family colonial palace, this excellent museum hosts temporary exhibitions mostly featuring contemporary Cuban artists but also great world masters. Cuba's most famous painter, Wilfredo Lam, directed most of his work to a non-Latin American audience. Born of Chinese and African ancestry, he blended synthetic cubism and African masks and surrealism to create an essentially Cuban vision.

Museo de Arqueología

Tacón 12 entre O'Reilly y Empedrado, **T** 8614469. *Tue-Sat 0900-1430, Sun 0900-1300. US$1. Map 6, B4, p256*

Originally built in the 17th century, the house was redesigned in 1725 by Juana Carvajal, a freed slave who inherited the building from her owner Lorenza Carvajal. In 1748, it was acquired and expanded by the Calvo de la Puerta family. It was restored and converted into a museum in 1988. Exhibitions are dedicated to colonial archaeological findings from La Habana Vieja and the bay and a collection of Cuban and Peruvian aboriginal artefacts.

Handicraft market and Castillo de la Punta

Tacón. *Behind Plaza de la Catedral and running parallel to the Av del Puerto, is Tacón, the setting for the old town's artisan market. Daily except Wed.* Map 6, 4A, p256 and Map 2, F6, p248 (See also p186)

All manner of not so cheap and cheerful tat is for sale, but you can pick up some good examples of Cuban pop art. Running northwest along the coast, Calle Tacón leads to the **Castillo de la Punta**. Built at the end of the 16th century, this is a squat building with 250 cm thick walls. Opposite the fortress, across the Malecón, is the Monumento a Máximo Gómez, the 19th-century independence leader.

Museo Nacional de la Música

Capdevila (Cárcel) 1 entre Habana y Aguiar, **T** 8619046. *Tue-Sat 1000-1745. US$2, US$1 with guide, photos US$3, video US$10. Map 2, G6, 249*

Fronting the Monumento a Máximo Gómez, this small and beautifully furnished old mansion houses an interesting collection of African drums, violins, musical gadgets and instruments from all around the world. Engaging exhibits chart the development of Cuban son and danzón and other musical styles between the 16th and 21st centuries. The museum hosts regular *peñas de nueva trova* featuring Marta Campos, Augusto Blanco and Alberto Tosca. On the last Thursday of the month there are evening *peñas de Tango* and on the last Friday, a *peña campesino,* which draws a mix of appreciative tourists and a buoyant local crowd. Admission depends on the performance, call ahead for times and prices.

> **!** Sugar was first introduced to Cuba by Christopher Columbus, who brought sugar cane roots from the Canary Islands on his second transatlantic voyage.

★ Castillo del Morro

Casablanca, T 8637941. *Daily 0830-2030 (museum 0900-2030). US$1 for the parque, US$3 for the castillo, under 12s free, US$1 guide, US$2 for photographs and US$2 for the lighthouse. Access to the castle is from any bus going through the tunnel (20 or 40 centavos). Board at San Lázaro and Av del Puerto and get off at the stop after the tunnel, cross the road and climb following the path to the left. Alternatively take a taxi, or a 20-min walk from the Fortaleza de San Carlos de la Cabaña (see Casablanca, p42). 10-peso colectivos depart from in front of Capitolio, but you will usually have to wait for one to fill up. Map 2, E7, p248*

The castle, also known as El Castillo de los Tres Reyes, was built between 1589 and 1630, with a 20-m moat, but has been much altered. It stands on a bold headland, with the best view of Havana and is illuminated at night. It was one of the major fortifications built to protect the natural harbour and the assembly of Spain's silver fleets from pirate attack. The beam of its lighthouse, built in 1844, is visible 30 km out to sea. It now serves as a museum with a good exhibition of Cuban history since the arrival of Columbus. Exhibits include skulls, bottles and remains of the *USS Maine* found in the bay, see p84. On the harbour side, down by the water, is the Battery of the 12 Apostles. Every night at 2100-2200, there is Spanish dancing and music. There is also a rather touristy disco, playing taped music at the *El Polvorín* bar; it's worth a visit for the views of the harbour and the whole of Havana.

Fortaleza de San Carlos de la Cabaña

T 8620617. *Daily 0900-2200. US$3 (0900-1800), US$5 (1800-2100), extra charge for camera or video. Map 2, H8, p249*

It is said that around 1590, the military engineer, Juan Bautista Antonelli, who built La Punta and El Morro, walked up the hill called La Cabaña one day and declared that "he who is master of this hill will be master of Havana". His prophecy was proved correct two centuries later when the English attacked Havana, conquering La Cabaña and thereby gaining control of the port. In 1763, after the English withdrew, another military engineer, Silvestre Abarca, arrived with a plan to build a fortress there. Construction lasted until 1774, when the fortress (the largest the Spanish had built until then in the Americas) was named San Carlos de la Cabaña, in honour of the king of Spain. It has a solid vertical wall of about 700 m with a deep moat connected to that of El Morro. In its heyday it had 120 cannons.

Inside are Los Fosos de los Laureles where political prisoners were shot during the Cuban fight for independence. On 3 January 1959, Che Guevara took possession of the fortress on his triumphant arrival in Havana after the flight of the dictator, Batista. Every night, the cannons are fired in an historical ceremony recalling the closure of the city walls to protect the city from attack by pirates. This used to happen at various times and originally in the 17th century the shot was fired from a naval ship in the harbour. Now, it is fired from La Cabaña at 2100 by soldiers in 18th-century uniforms, with the ceremony starting at 2045. There are two museums here: one about Che Guevara and another about fortresses with pictures and models, some old weapons and a replica of a large catapult and battering ram from the 16th to 18th centuries. If you go up the fort to the far wall, stand on the parapet and look over, you can see two missiles below on the outside of the wall, pointing out to sea. Access as for Castillo del Morro, see above, or via Casablanca.

Casablanca

Take the left-hand ferry queue for Casablanca next to the Customs House, opposite Santa Clara, 10 centavos. Map 2, I8, p249

The National Observatory and the former railway station (Hershey line) for trains to Matanzas are on the same side of the channel as these two forts. This charming town is also the site of a white marble statue of Jesus Christ, which overlooks Havana harbour. It was erected during the Batista dictatorship as a pacifying exercise. You can get a good view of Havana's skyline from Parque El Cristo, particularly at night, but be careful not to miss the last ferry back. Go up a steep, twisting flight of stone steps, starting on the other side of the plaza in front of the landing stage. There is a *Rumbos* café here, popular with young couples. You can walk from the statue to the Fortaleza (10 minutes) and then on to the Castillo del Morro.

Farmacia Taquechel

Obispo 155 entre Mercaderes y San Ignacio, **T** 8629286.
Map 6, C3, p256

Restored in the mid 1990s, and primed for tourism, the Taquechel pharmacy seduces passers-by with its medicinal artistry and heady, pungent aromas. All manner of natural herbs, remedies and hocus pocus concoctions are stored in porcelain jars, glazed and gilded with herbal motifs and symbols of longevity, and then meticulously arranged on floor to ceiling polished mahogany shelves. The original 1896 construction was the workplace of Francisco Taquechel Mirabal.

Estudio Galería Rigoberto Mena

San Ignacio 154 entre Obispo y Obrapía, **T** 8675884.
Map 6, D3, p256

Another of Cuba's most respected contemporary artists, Mena's studio just off Obispo houses a fantastic collection of abstract art. Influenced by the likes of Jackson Pollock and Geogwa Mathieu, his universal style has received critical acclaim world-wide. Mena's style is deceptively simple, a poetic and meticulous composition of brilliant colours radiating from dark backgrounds. The artist is usually on hand to discuss his work, and with very affordable smaller lithographs and canvases, it is well worth dropping in.

Casa de Simón Bolívar

Mercaderes 158 entre Obrapía y Lamparilla, **T** 8613988. *Tue-Sat 0930-1700, Sun 0930-1300. US$1. Map 6, E3, p256*

This thoughtfully constructed museum space presents in vivid detail the life of the South American liberator, Simón de Bolívar.The upstairs galleries are devoted to both Cuban and Venezuelan art and Colombian photography exhibitions.

La Casa de la Obra-Pía

Obrapía 158 entre Mercaderes y San Ignacio, **T** 8613097. *Tue-Sat 0900-1630, Sun 0930-1230. Photos US$2. Map 6, D3, p256*

Built in 1665, this beautiful yellow building now houses a furniture museum. The house was remodelled in 1793 by the Marqués de Cárdenas de Monte Hermoso, whose shield is over the door. The portico was made in Cádiz in 1793, but finished off in Havana. The building was restored in 1983, but work still continue on the upper floors. The museum contains furniture from the 18th and 19th centuries, including collections from Asia and displays of Cuban medals and thrones. There is an interesting exhibition, of the life of Alejo Carpentier, see p222. The collection includes photos of his imprisonment in 1927 for petitioning against the Machado government. Carpentier escaped on a false passport to Paris, where he lived between 1928-39. He was one of the few writers to gain favour with the Castro government. The **Fundación Alejo Carpentier** houses a collection of the writer's letters and books. Empedrado 215 entre Cuba y San Ignacio, Monday to Friday 0830-1630. Free but donations are welcome.

! Calle Obrapía, meaning pious deed, was named after the benefactor Don Martín Calvo de la Puerta, who took up the worthy cause of providing dowries to five orphaned girls each year, keeping many a potential Havana spinster off the shelf.

★ Havana film moments

Best

- Coppelia, p139 and p 81.
- La Guardia, p133.
- Salón Rojo, p161.
- El Malecón, p56.
- Hotel Sevilla, p107.

Casa de Africa

Obrapía 157 entre San Ignacio y Mercaderes, **T** 8615798, africa@cultural.ohch.cu *Mon-Sat 1030-1700, Sun 0930-1300. US$2, under 12s free. Map 6, D3, p256*

Undergoing renovation until the beginning of 2003, many of the exhibits from this museum can be seen at Museo Humboldt, see p46. A must for anyone on the Afro trail, the museum provides an engaging insight into the spectrum of African culture and religion in Cuba. It houses a collection of Afro-Cuban religious artefacts collected by the late Don Fernando Ortíz, the founding father of Afro-Cuban ethnological studies.

Casa de Guayasimín

Obrapía 111 entre Mercaderes y Oficios, **T** 8613843. *Tue-Sat 0930-1630, Sun 0930-1430. Donations welcome. Map 6, E4, p256*

Exhibition of works donated to Cuba by the late Ecuadorean artist Oswaldo Guayasimín, including paintings, sculptures and silk-screens. Guayasimín painted a famous portrait of Fidel with his hands raised for his 70th birthday. Temporary exhibitions are held on the second floor and you can visit the artist's private rooms. There is a great shop on the ground floor, with separate access, which provides a good initiation into his life and work.

Museo Humboldt

Oficios 254 esquina Muralla, **T** 8639850. *Mon-Sat 0800-1700, Sun 0800-1300. Free. Map 6, G4, p256*

Explorer and botanist Federico Enrique Alejandro von Humboldt (1769-1857) lived here in 1801 when he completed his calculations of the latitude and longitude of Havana. Humboldt paved the way for Charles Darwin, who called him the greatest naturalist of his time. The museum contains reproductions of the plants and insects he collected during his extensive travels in Latin America, and the desk of Fernando Ortíz, Humboldt's first editor.

Galería de Arte Carmen Montilla Tinoco

Oficios entre Armagura y Teniente Rey, **T** 338768. *Tue-Sat 0930-1445, Sun 0900-1300. Map 6, F4, p256*

The house dates from the beginning of the 18th century. The Oficina del Historiador, with the help of the Venezuelan artist and close friend of Fidel, restored it after a fire in the 1980s, and opened it as an art gallery in her name in 1994, dedicated to Cuban and international art exhibitions. The high point of the museum is the stunning ceramic mural by Alfredo Sosabravo, a vivid evocation of the flora and fauna of the Caribbean, in the patio garden.

● *Close by, on Plaza de Simón Bolívar, there is colourful mural painted by Tinoco, dedicated to Eusebio Leal. It is one of many public art space masterpieces in Havana.*

Casa de los Arabes

Oficios 16 entre Obispo and Obrapía, **T** 8615868. *0930-1630, US$1, photos US$2. Map 6, D4, p256*

This lovely colonial building built in the Mudéjar style, with red-brick arcades, ornate balconies, intricate ceilings and a vine-trailed courtyard, is a clear example of the Moorish influence on Cuban architecture. The collection includes everything from sparkling jewels, gold and silver plated weapons from the 18th and 19th centuries, rugs, Saharan robes, model reproductions of traditional sailboats and a replica souk.The only mosque in Havana is found here, and includes a Koran and other religious artefacts. The inner courtyard of the adjoining *Restaurante Al Medina* is a tranquil spot for a relaxing lunch and some tasty Arab food, see p131.

Museo de Automóviles
Oficios 12 y Jústiz, just off Plaza de Armas, **T** 8615062.
Daily 0900-1900, US$1.   Map 6, D5, p256

The vintage car museum showcases cars dating back to the 1920s, lovingly maintained with 90% of their original parts, and still with plenty of cruising potential. However, many that would have been exhibits in other museums around the world are still working machines - around 155,000 pre-revolutionary vehicles, including Buiks, Lincolns, Mercurys, Chevys and Chryslers, still belch and splutter their way through the streets of Havana. This museum is due to move at the end of 2002.

La Casa Benito Juárez (Casa de México)
Obrapía 116 entre Mercaderes y Oficios, **T** 8618166.
Tue-Sat 0930-1730, Sun 0900-1300.   Map 6, D4, p256

Overlooking Plaza de Simón Bolívar in the heart of spruced up Havana, the Mexican museum is housed in a pearly-pink 18th-century building, draped with the Mexican flag. More of a cultural centre than a museum, the meagre and rather unspectacular exhibits include pre-Columbian artefacts and popular arts and crafts drawn from 18 Mexican states, including ceramics from Jalisco. If you are waning, a convenient pit stop next door is the *Cafetería Torrelavega* for cheap sustenance, see p132.

Galería Los Oficios,
Oficios 166 entre Amargura y Teniente Rey, **T** 339804
Tue-Sun 1000-1700. Map 6, F4, p256

Nelsón Domínguez is one of the most revered and prolific of
contemporary Cuban artists. Working in various mediums, he is
primarily influenced by the natural environment and draws heavily
on indigenous and spiritual symbolism, providing provocative and
emotive insights into the Cuban psyche. The highlight of the
gallery is the homage to Hemingway, a wacky typewriter
installation surrounded by unmistakable symbols of Big Ern.

Museo Numismático
Oficios 8 entre Obispo y Obrapía, **T** 8615811. *Tue-Sat
1000-1600, Sun 0900-1300. Free. Map 6, D5, p256*

The coin museum exhibits and sells money, medals and
numismatic documentation. The extensive collection of more
than 1,000 pieces, including rare notes and valuable gold
coins, dates from the colonial period up to the Revolution.

Museo Histórico de las Ciencias Carlos J Finlay
Cuba 460 entre Amargura y Brasil, **T** 8634824. *Mon-Fri
0800-1700, Sat 0900-1500. US$1. Map 6, E2, p256*

Carlos J Finlay was an eminent Cuban doctor who discovered that
the mosquito was the vector of yellow fever in the late 19th century and helped to eradicate the disease in Cuba. The museum
contains exhibits on the development of science in Cuba.

!
The first car appeared on the roads in 1898. Manufactured
by French company, *La Parisiense*, it reached, at full throttle,
a trotting speed of 12 km per hour. It was a snip at 1000 pesos
– not much more than the price of a horse and cart.

★ **Stops on the Afro Trail**

Best

- Sábado de la Rumba sessions, p157.
- The Casa de África, p45.
- Museo Municipal de Regla, p95.
- Callejón Hamel, p68.
- Museo Municipal de Guanabacoa, p96.

Havana

Plaza de San Francisco de Asís
Map 6, F4, p256

Heading south from Plaza de Armas, Calle Oficios opens out onto the wide, cobbled square of San Francisco de Asís. On the north side of the square stands the stocky neoclassical Cuban Stock Exchange building, La Lonja. Built at the beginning of the 20th century, it was renovated in 1996 to provide office space. Facing onto the plaza is the Terminal de Sierra Maestra, where luxury liners dock and visitors come ashore. Dominating the southern parameter, and adding a spiritual allure to the square's otherwise soulless practicality, is the church and convent of San Francisco de Asís.

Iglesia y Convento de San Francisco de Asís
Plaza de San Francisco de Asís. *Daily 0930-1830. US$2 for museum and bell tower, photos US$2, video US$10, guide US$1. Tickets for concerts are sold 3 days in advance. Map 6, F4, p256*

Built in 1608 and rebuilt in baroque style in 1730, this is a massive, sombre edifice, suggesting defence, rather than worship. The three-storey bell tower (*campanario*) was both a landmark for returning voyagers and a look-out for pirates and has stunning views of the city and port. When the 40-m tower was added, it became the highest religious building in Latin America. No longer a church, only the exterior of the building, in particular the Escorial

There's much of the voyeur in those gazers in the street. In Havana one is used to looking at faces, bodies, the way a tourist examines a monument, sometimes even more brazenly. The *habanero* looks at faces with his whole heart and soul.

Eyes of Havana, *Aperture*, Issue 141, 1995
Antonio José Aponte

style of the façade, retains the baroque splendour. The Basílica Menor de San Francisco de Asís is now a concert hall and the convent is a museum containing religious pieces.

The church contains the remains of the eccentric fantasy figure of El Caballero de París (French Wanderer). The story of this distinguished vagrant is legendary in Havana; Juan Manuel López Lledín was a Galícian immigrant who came to Cuba in the second half of the 20th century. Mad as a hatter, with cloak billowing, wild locks of hair and a deluded sense of grandeur, he was embraced affectionately by *habaneros*. Working as a waiter in many of Cuba's top hotels, including the *Telégrafo* and the *Sevilla*, his notoriety spread throughout the capital. Legend has it that Lledín's madness sprang either from his being falsely imprisoned for theft, or through pining for his forsaken love in Galícia. Lledín died in Havana's psychiatric hospital in 1985, aged 95. The sculpture of Lledín, in front of the church, was the work of José Villa, who also sculpted the John Lennon monument in Vedado, see p78.

El Jardín de Diana
Baratillo, near Plaza San Francisco. *0700-1900*. *Map 6, E5, p256*

The British Embassy financed the construction of the memorial garden for Diana, Princess of Wales. This curious shrine surrounded by shrubbery is dominated by a tall concrete tube covered in ceramics in the shape of liquorice all-sorts, which don't quite reach to the top, symbolizing a life cut short. There is also a sculpture of

! It is said one of Hemingway's drinking buddies, composer Fernando Campoamor and the owner of *La Bodeguita del Medio*, together concocted what must be one of the most lucrative tourist cons ever. They hired a calligrapher to write the line "Mi mojito en La Bodeguita, Mi daiquirí en El Floridita", over the bar in *La Bodeguita*. Big Ern's style it may have been, his authentic signature it wasn't.

the sun, representing the happiness in her life, but one triangle is missing, representing her heart. Around the base of the pole are rings symbolising sadness. There is a caretaker there who will be happy to explain the symbolism to visitors.

La Plaza Vieja
Map 6, F2, p256

Heading west from Plaza de San Francisco de Asís, along Brasil (Teniente Rey), is the 18th-century Plaza Vieja. Essentially a residential domain of colonial baroque mansions and apartments, it suffered from years of neglect. During the 18th century, the square was the setting for all manner of giddy and gruesome stately events from jovial fiestas to bloody executions and bullfights. In 1952 Batista left his own philistine legacy by constructing an underground car park, which destroyed the original centrepiece stone fountain. The square is undergoing restoration as part of a project by UNESCO and Habaguanex, the state company responsible for the restoration of La Habana Vieja. A clutch of minor museums and galleries is now housed in the colonial residences, and a replica of the original fountain has been returned to centre stage. The *Fototeca de Cuba* showcases international photography exhibitions in one of the converted mansions. On the north side of the square, on Teniente Rey, is the swanky, but very overpriced restaurant, *Santo Angel*, and on the east side, on Inquisidor, the old post office, dating from 1909, is being renovated.

Centro de las Artes Visuales
La Casona, Muralla 107, Plaza Vieja esquina San Ignacio,
T 8618544, www.artnet.com/casona *Map 6, F2, p256*

The former house of the Spanish Captain General, Conde de Ricla, who retook Havana from the English and restored power to Spain in 1763, is now known as La Casona. Modern art exhibitions are held upstairs in the charming blue and white building. Check out the friezes up the staircase and along the walls. There is a great view of the plaza from the balcony and plants in the courtyard enhance the atmosphere.

Museo de Naipes

Plaza Vieja, Muralla 101, **T** 8601534. *Tue-Sat 0900-1445, Sun 0900-1300. Donations welcome. Map 6, G2, p256*

This rather quirky card museum is very popular with groups of schoolchildren and worth a gander. More than 2,000 cards are colourfully presented on a rotating basis, ranging from collections of Japanese comic all stars and intricate 16th-century Persian and Russian playing cards to Maya symbolism reproductions and nifty card miniatures of Miró and Kandinsky masterpieces. There are also Spanish caricatures, including Woody Allen, and tarot cards. A display of engraving and production materials and, slightly more off base, 19th-century cigar *anillas* (wrappers), complete the collection.

Museo del Ron

Av del Puerto 262 entre Sol y Muralla, **T** 8618051, www.havanaclubfoundation.com *Daily 0900-1700. US$5, under 15s free, multilingual guides included. Map 6, H4, p256*

The Fundación Distilería Havana Club has a well-laid out museum offering displays of the production of rum from the sugar cane plantation to the processing and bottling, with machinery dating from the early 20th century. A replica distillery, with barrels of bubbling booze, this is an enjoyably atmospheric initiation into the production process of Havana's top tipple. The highlight of the tour is a wonderful model railway, which runs round a model sugar mill and distillery, designed and made by prize-winning Lázaro Eduardo García Driggs in 1993-94 and restored in 1999-2000. On the downside, the museum is too dark in places to read the notices and the

poor sound quality of the video films can be difficult to understand.
The tour guides here also tend to be the fastest in the west. If your
Spanish is up to it, take the native tongue tour. The finale is a tasting
of six-year-old *Havana Club* rum in the cellar-style bar, a mock up of
the once-famous *Sloppy Joe's*. There is also a restaurant and shop
selling special edition *Havana Club*. Each month all visitors are
entered into a lottery for the rum lover's dream prize, a bottle of
25-year-old *San Cristóbal Havana Club*.

Convento de Santa Clara

Occupies four small blocks in La Habana Vieja, bounded by Calles
Habana, Sol, Cuba and Luz. *Mon-Fri 0900-1500. US$2 for guided
tour in Spanish or French. Map 6, G1, p256*

The convent was founded in 1644 by nuns from Cartagena, Colombia. It was in use as a convent until 1919, when the nuns sold the
building. In a shady business deal it was later acquired by the
government and, after radical alterations, it became offices for the
Ministry of Public Works until the decision was made to restore the
building. Originally there were three cloisters and an orchard. You
can see the cloisters, the cemetery and their cells.

The ground floor is a grand porticoed stone gallery surrounding a large patio packed with vegetation. In it are the city's first
slaughterhouse, first public fountain and public baths. The
Sailor's House in the second cloister, reputedly built by a sailor for
his lovelorn daughter, is now a Residencia Académica for student
groups (and independent travellers if room, see Sleeping, p112).
The convent is topped by a tiled roof with a stone turret next to the
church choir.

There is a great, well-stocked, listen-before-you-commit CD shop,
which also has lots of must-see Cuban films to buy, including many
of Tomás Gutiérrez Alea's seminal works.

► El Jefe

Now in his mid-seventies, Fidel Castro, *jefe* (chief) and supreme comandante of Cuba, has passed from being the world's youngest ruler in 1959 to the longest-serving head of state. He has outstayed eight US presidents and survived hundreds of assassination attempts. It is reported he still exercises regularly and works long hours, but his speeches are now shorter and less passionate. His longest speech lasted seven hours, but Cubans were regularly called upon to listen to his rhetoric for five hours.

Fidel, who has always been instantly recognizable for his beard, and his military fatigues, was born in 1926 and became a lawyer before taking up the revolutionary cause. His first armed uprising with 150 insurgents was launched on the Moncada barracks in Santiago de Cuba on 26 July 1953. The attack was repelled, rebels were killed and others including Castro faced 15 years' imprisonment. When dictator Batista amnestied political prisoners in 1955, Castro chose exile. Later, in Mexico, he met Che Guevara. From there he launched his second incursion, sailing on the *Granma*, and landing in Cuba on 2 December 1956, with over 80 men. The uprising was crushed by the military, but 12 men, including Castro, escaped into the mountains. There they organized the 26 July Movement beginning with guerrilla warfare while building up popular support.

Although his brother Raúl was a Marxist-Leninist, Fidel campaigned on a nationalist platform and only later turned to communism. On 17 March 1958 he called for a general revolt. His popularity and forces had grown steadily and they pushed on to Havana. On 1 January 1959 Batista fled the country and a provisional government was established. Castro renounced office, but was prevailed upon to become prime minister and later president.

Museo Casa Natal de José Martí

Leonor Pérez 314 entre Picota y Egido, opposite central railway station, **T** 8613778. *Tue-Sat 0900-1700, Sun 0900-1300. US$1.*
Map 2, L4, p249

The birthplace of Cuba's greatest hero, José Martí, this modest house has been devoted to his memory since a plaque was first put on the wall in 1899. A museum since 1925, restored in 1952-53, it presents the full life story of the man who dedicated his life to the liberation of Cuba from Spanish colonial rule. The rich complexity of this national hero, whose powerful words are frequently invoked by Fidel, is documented with photos, mementoes, furniture and papers.

Centro

Cosmetically a war zone, the residential district of Centro captivates with its animated streets and combustible ethnic composite. Begin-ning on the western corner of Parque Central is **El Prado***, a leafy boulevard punctuated with bronze lions and baroque lamp posts. Flanked by flaking stately mansions, and set to a more tranquil tempo, it oozes an ageing beauty. This is where locals saunter rather than strut, kids skateboard rather than hustle, and tourists soak up the clinging aura of the belle époque.*

Where the Prado ends, the **Malecón** *begins. Snaking around from La Punta to Vedado, the Malecón is Havana's seafront esplanade, beguiling, poetic and invigorating. Where the ocean crashes dramatically across the sea wall, craggy, salt-encrusted fishermen stoop, lovers meet, and clusters of boys dive off the rocks below. Across the six-lane highway stands an architectural panoply of buildings, ravaged by time, and eroded by salt.*

Centro's main artery is **Calle San Rafael***, which runs west from Parque Central. Clogged with humanity, it pulsates with a cacophony of barking dogs, cackling women and pounding salsa. Havana's 19th-century retail playground, it is spliced by ramshackle streets, strewn* with rubble and lined with decrepit houses, choking in the sulphurous stench of vintage US cars as they rumble through the streets. At the cross-section of Amistad and Dragones stands the gateway to **Barrio Chino**, a perplexing Cuban-Chinese hybrid. In its pre-Revolutionary heyday, this ten-block zone, pivoting around the Cuchillo de Zanja, was an opium-hazed pleasure zone of sordid theatres and steamy brothels. Now, a glut of restaurants strewn with lanterns, a colourful food market, and a smattering of Chinese associations, are all that remains of what was the largest Chinatown in Latin America.

A shrine to pleasures pagan and divine, the derelict barrio of **Cayo Hueso** lies in the triangle between Infanta, San Lázaro and the Malecón. Entrenched in Santería and energised by a rich artistic spirit, it beats to an electrifying crescendo of rumba. Rising from these rough-hewn alleyways, once crumbling apartments have been reincarnated as living artworks, their sickly façades painted with kaleidoscopic murals.

» *See Sleeping, p112, Eating and drinking, p133, Bars and clubs, p154.*

Havana

◉ Sights

★ **Parque Central**
Map 2, I4, p249

All roads seem to lead to the elegant central park, a 24-hour entertainment and transport hub, and the launch pad onto the tourist merry-go-round of La Habana Vieja. Surrounded by whizzing traffic, it is an eye-popping medley of social activity and majestic architecture. Populated with mojito-merry tourists, Parque Central is a quick-buck Mecca for every hustler, offering every carnal pleasure in the book. Jockeying for tourist attention, cavorting minstrels deliver routine renditions of the catchy *Guantanamera*, Havana's quintessential tourist bait tune. Flanking the park's parameters, Havana's myriad transport options, vintage US Chevys, horse-drawn carriages,

57

yellow cocotaxis and bicitaxis, surreally clustered in a technological time warp. The monument in Parque Central is dedicated to José Martí. On the southeastern corner is the *Rincón Caliente* (hot corner), a kind of speaker's corner where Havana's aspiring orators launch into heated debate over the serious subject of baseball. On the north side, chilling out to a more mellow beat is Havana's Rasta community, mingling on the marble benches, in the shade of *poincianas*, laurels and Royal Palms.

Occupying this entire north side is the much-derided *Hotel Golden Tulip*, considered by many *habaneros* to be an affront to La Habana Vieja's colonial splendour. The *Hotel Plaza* is in the northeast corner, and on the west side is the newly renovated *Hotel Telégrafo*, flanked by the historic *Hotel Inglaterra*. This hotel's pavement café, *El Louvre*, built in 1843, predates the hotel, and provided a meeting spot for Havana's revolutionary youth during Spanish colonial rule.

On the eastern side is the unmissable Museo Nacional de Bellas Artes (see p 60), with a creamy clean façade. The Parque Central's architectural zenith is the majestic **Gran Teatro de la Habana**, a whimsical neo-baroque monument dating from 1838. It is used by the national opera and also houses the Teatro García Lorca. Sarah Bernhardt once performed here when the Teatro García Lorca was called the Teatro Tacón. Tours of the theatre can be arranged, but for a finer appreciation of architecture and the aura, the best option is attend a performance; details are posted in the entrance, tickets cost US$5-10.

★ El Prado
Map 2, H4-F6, p248-249

Skirting the western side of Parque Central is El Paseo de Martí, commonly known as El Prado. Leading down to the Malecón, it technically divides La Habana Vieja and Centro Habana. In the mid-19th century this serene, tree-lined boulevard was a polarized world of slave dwellings and sumptuous mansions. Aristocratic ladies made their customary jaunt along the walkway, punctuated with bronze lions and ornate lamp posts, surveying the theatrics of the masses from the splendour of their carriages. Nowadays, locals stroll or linger on the benches under the laurel trees, kids play baseball and local artists paint and proffer their work to passing tourists. Renovation work is returning the colourful residential buildings, fronted with pillars, to their former glory. Despite the peeling paint, cavernous interiors and strewn washing, this architectural panoply oozes belle époque magnificence.

★ Museo de la Revolución
Refugio entre Monserrate y Zulueta, facing Av las Misiones.
T 624091/6. *Daily 1000-1800. US$4, guided tour 1030, US$10, recommended, cameras allowed, US$1 extra. Allow several hours, explanations are mostly in Spanish.   Map 2, G6, p249*

One of Havana's premier attractions, this museum is audaciously housed in the former presidential palace. It charts, in often over-whelming detail, and with vivid iconography, the history of Cuban political development from slave uprisings to joint space missions with the ex-Soviets. Built in 1920, the huge, ornate building, topped by a dome, was home to more than 20 Cuban presidents before it was transformed into a museum in 1974. The lavish interior was designed by Tiffany of New York. The liveliest section displays the final battles against Batista's troops, with excellent photographs and some bizarre personal mementoes, such as a revolutionary's knife, fork and spoon, and a shower curtain worn in the Sierra Maestra campaign. Look out for the bullet holes as you walk up the stairs.

At the top of the main staircase are a stuffed mule and a stuffed horse used by Che and Camilo Cienfuegos in the same campaign. The yacht *Granma*, from which Castro disembarked with his companions in 1956 to launch the Revolution, has been installed in the park facing the south entrance, surrounded by planes, tanks and other vehicles involved, as well as a Soviet-built tank used against the Bay of Pigs invasion and a fragment from a US spy plane shot down in the 1970s.

★ Museo Nacional de Bellas Artes, Palacio de Bellas Artes

The Arte Cubano is at Trocadero entre Zulueta y Monserrate. The Arte Universal is at San Rafael entre Zulueta y Monserrate, both **T** 8613858/620140, www.museonacional.cult.cu *Tue-Sat 1000-1800, Sun 0900-1300. Both museums cost US$5, but a same day entrance to both sites is US$8, reduced rates for children and students, no photography permitted. Map 2, H5, p249 and I4, p249*

An exceptional museum, the Museum of Fine Arts is essential viewing for anyone interested in colonial and modern art and well worth a look even if you are not a keen art buff. The art collection is valued at more than US$500 million and consists of 47,628 works of art, from an ancient Egyptian sarcophagus to contemporary Cuban paintings. The exhibits are divided between the original 1954 museum in Trocadero, housing the Cuban art collection from colonial times to the 1990s including a section on the post-Revolution Art Schools, and the former Centro Asturiano, housing European and ancient art.

Cuban art collection Start on the third floor with the colonial art and work your way down to the present day. Colonial art, spanning the 17th-19th century, is separated into four sections devoted to religious and landscape paintings and portraits. There are portraits by José Nicolás de la Escalera (1734-1804) and Victor Patricio Landaluze and 19th-century landscape paintings by Frederico Fernández Cavada. The high point is Victor Manuel's sensational painting *Gitana Tropical*. See Art, p220. There are representations of modern-era Cuban paintings from René Portocarrero and Wilfredo Lam, Cuba's most famous painter. After living for many

Colonial character

Vintage American cars and wrought iron-encrusted apartment buildings make up the urban fabric of La Habana Vieja.

years in Spain and France, he was encouraged to explore primitive art by the Parisian art circle, including, Picasso, André Bréton and Benjamin Péret. The diverse influences upon Cuban art during the 1940s are apparent in the work of Amelia Peláez and Carlos Enríquez. The influence of the colourful murals of Mexico can be seen in the striking *Naturaleza Muerta Con Piña, Flores Amarillas* and *Pez*. Cuba's answer to Andy Warhol, pop artist Raúl Martínez (1927-95), is well represented. Rather than featuring the capitalist and 60s iconography of its US counterpart, Cuban pop art, not surprisingly, was inspired by the ubiquitous images of revolution-aries. Exhibited works of more recent Cuban artists include those of Roberto Fabelo, Zaida del Río and Alfredo Sosabravo.

The International collection The colonial building designed by the Spanish architect Manuel del Busto in the early 20th century, has been fabulously renovated with huge marble staircases giving access to five floors. The large collection of European paintings, from the 16th century to the present, contains works by Gainsborough, Van Dyck, Velázquez, Tintoretto, Degas, et al. One painting by Canaletto, in the Italian room on the fifth floor, is in fact only half a painting; the other half of the 18th-century painting *Chelsea from the Thames* is owned by the National Trust in Britain and hangs in Blickling Hall, Norfolk. It is believed to have been commissioned in 1746-48 by the Chelsea Hospital, which is featured in the Cuban half, but the artist was unable to sell it and cut it in two just before he died in 1768. The left half was sold to the 11th Marquis of Lothian, whose family owned Blickling Hall, where it has stayed ever since. The right half was bought and sold several times until it ended up with a Cuban collector, Oscar Cinetas, who donated it to the museum before the Revolution.

The museum also has Greek, Roman, Egyptian and Etruscan sculpture and artefacts, many very impressive. The unharmed Greek amphora from the 5th century BC is considered remarkable. The museum also includes paintings from private collections left behind by rich Cuban families (including the Bacardí and Gómez Mena families) and members of the former dictator Fulgencio Batista's government who fled Cuba soon after the 1959 Revolution. The origin of these works, including Spanish artists Sorolla and Zurbarán, has been included in the catalogues. It had been rumoured that some of these collections had been sold by the Cuban government during the economic crisis of the Special Period. Additionally, there are rooms dedicated to Latin American art and 18th- and 19th-century paintings from the United States.

Parque Fraternidad
Map 2, J3, p249

The park was originally called Parque de Colón, but was renamed to mark the VI Panamerican Conference in 1892. It has been landscaped to show off the Capitolio, north of it, to the best effect. At its centre is a *ceiba* tree growing in soil provided by each of the American republics. Also in the park is a famous statue of the Amerindian woman who first welcomed the Spaniards: La Noble Habana, sculpted in 1837. From the southwest corner the handsome Avenida Allende runs due west to the high hill, on which stands El Príncipe Castle (now the city gaol). The *Quinta de los Molinos*, on this avenue, at the foot of the hill, once housed the School of Agronomy of Havana University. The main house now contains the Máximo Gómez museum (Dominican Republic-born fighter for Cuban independence). Also here is the headquarters of the association of young writers and artists (Asociación Hermanos Saiz). The gardens are a lovely place to stroll. North, along Calle Universidad, on a hill that gives a good view, is the university.

! The white dome over a rotunda inside the Capitolio is 62 m high and inside there is a 17-m statue of Jupiter, symbol of liberty, which represents the republic. This is the tallest interior statue in Latin America and the third largest in the world.

Capitolio

Paseo de Martí entre San Martín y Dragones, T 610261. *0900-2000 but often shuts early, US$3 to go in the halls, tours available, camera and video charge US$2. Entrance for visitors is to the left of the stairway.* Map 2, I3, p249

Gracefully dominating the Havana skyline, the Capitolio serves as an ironic reminder of US neocolonialism. It was built in the style of the US Capitol in Washington DC by the dictator Machado in 1926-29 an attempt to impress his US paymasters with his loyalty. It was initially used as the seat of parliament for the Senate and the House of Representatives before they were dissolved after the Revolution.

A 24-carat replica diamond is set into the centre of the floor of the exquisite entrance hall, which pinpoints zero for all distance measurements in Cuba. The interior has large halls and stately staircases, all lavishly decorated. The Salón de las Pasos Perdidos (Hall of Lost Steps) is embellished almost entirely with marble, and drips with exquisite copper and bronze detailing. It was the custom following the Revolution to turn emblems of neocolonialism over for public benefit; the Capitolio now houses the Cuban Academy of Sciences and the National Library of Science and Technology. There is a restaurant and café overlooking the park and an internet café, see Directory, p201.

Partagás

Industria 520 entre Dragones y Barcelona, behind the Capitolio, T 338060. *Tours every 15 mins 0930-1200, 1330-1500, US$10, English, Spanish or French speaking guides available. Shop and bar, 0900-1700.* Map 2, I3, p249

This interesting, if rather pricey, 30-minute tour of the cigar factory unfortunately destroys the erotic myth that cigars are rolled on the thighs of dusky virgins. You are taken through the factory and shown the whole production process from the storage and sorting of the leaves, to rolling, banding, packaging, labelling and the final sealing with the government's guarantee. Following a nine-month course, the skilled *torcedores* are expected to roll around 100 cigars per day as they listen to daily press or novel readings, a tradition continued since 1865. A rigorous quality control is enforced by the not surprisingly nicotine-stained quality controller, at the end of the production line, with substandard cigars being returned to the original roller. Many different brand names are made here: *Partagás, Cohiba, Ramón Allones, Romeo y Julieta* and *Bolívar*. These and other famous cigars and rum can be bought at the shop here, credit cards accepted, where you can enjoy a sample smoke, with a cooling mojito in the bar. The lightest and cheapest option is the *Romeo y Julieta*, US$3.40 each, the strongest is the *Bolívar* and the finest, to be savoured at US$12.90 each, is the *Cohiba* – first created just for Fidel. Cigars are also made at many tourist locations, for example the Palacio de la Artesanía, see p154, the airport and at some of Havana's more upper-crust hotels.

Chinatown
Map 2, I3, p249

Just west of Capitolio, at the intersection of Amistad and Dragones, is Barrio Chino, once the largest Chinatown in Latin America. The first wave of Chinese immigrants came to Cuba in 1847, and by the end of the century there were more than 10,000 Chinese inhabiting a ten-block area. They suffered the same discrimination as Afro-Cubans, working on the sugar plantations under what the government termed as 'colonial contracting', to all intents and purposes, slaves. In the 1940s and 1950s, this murky warren of opium-hazed streets was the playground of America's hedonists. With a warp factor way beyond the titillation of today's cabarets, the notorious Shanghai Theatre featured live sex shows. Graham Greene who was all-too-familiar with the Havana underbelly,

Santería

With at least as many believers as the Roman Catholic Church in Cuba, Santería draws its support from all walks of life. Roman Catholicism has been traditionally shunned by the regime, and until 1992, Cuba was officially an atheist state. Traditionally associated with the upper-class elite, Castro has never taken kindly to the church's support of counter-revolutionaries. In contrast, the Revolution has been imbued with superstitions of an Afro-Cuban religion traditionally associated with the masses. When Fidel delivered his speech in the Plaza de La Revolución in 1959, a white dove landed on his shoulder, indicating he was the 'chosen one'.

Between the mid-16th century and late 19th century, African slaves brought to Cuba their customs and beliefs, which provided a shred of comfort in their traumatic new existence on the sugar plantations. The most influential group were the Yoruba-speaking agricult-uralists, known as *lucumí*. It is their pantheon of orishas (deities), and the legends (*pwatakis*) and customs surrounding these, which form the basis of the syncretic Regla de Ocha cult, or Santería. Though slaves were ostensibly obliged to become Christians, their owners, anxious to prevent different ethnic groups uniting, turned a blind eye to their traditional rituals. The Catholic saints thus spont-aneously syncretized in the *lucumí* mind with the orishas, whose imagined attributes they shared. For every orisha there is a code of conduct and dress to which his *hijos* must conform, and a series of rhythms played on *batá* drums. While the Yoruba recognize 400 or more regional or tribal orishas, their Cuban descendants have forgotten, discarded or fused together most of these, so that today barely two dozen regularly receive tribute at the rites known as *toques de santo*.

brought Wormwold here in *Our Man in Havana*. Following the Revolution, Chinatown's debauched excesses were curbed, or creatively concealed at least, and a mass exodus decimated the Chinese population. In the 1960s, a flurry of Chinese immigrants arrived from California and the area was rejuvenated. The revival was short lived, however, and it is estimated there are fewer than 500 pure bred Chinese left in Cuba. The entrance to Chinatown is marked by an immense gateway crowned with a pagoda-style roof, the largest of its kind in the world. Continuing south, the area commonly known as Cuchillo de Zanja is decked out with colourful lanterns strewn above a vibrant ensemble of cheap restaurants, some rather less salubrious than others, and peso stalls serving up glutinous concoctions in *cajas*, or takeaway boxes. Both Hemingway and Fidel were patrons of the *Pacífico* restaurant, unmissable in the guise of a Chinese temple, but unsatisfying in the quality of the not-so-Chinese gastronomy. There are vestiges of this once ebullient Chinatown; an excellent colourful peso food market, Chinese pharmacy, herbal shops, arts centre and newspaper.

Cayo Hueso
Map 3, H7, p251

Dating back to the beginning of the 20th century, Cayo Hueso is a run down barrio lying in a triangle between Infanta, San Lázaro and the Malecón. It was named by cigar factory workers returning from Key West and has nothing to do with bones (*huesos* in Spanish), although it was once the site of the Espada cemetery and the San Lázaro quarry. There are about 12,000 homes, mostly tenements, which have been earmarked for a slow-moving project to halt their deterioration. The project also involves educating the community in its own culture and history. In 1924, the factory workers built a place for their social activities on San Lázaro, which became the site of the José Martí People's University. San Lázaro, with the **Universidad de Havana**'s wide stairway at its top, was the site of fierce and determined student movement demonstrations from the late 1920s onwards. By the mid-1950s, Infanta was the Maginot line where the students faced Batista's troops.

● *In July 1953, Fidel Castro departed from Calle Jovellar 107 for the attack on the Moncada Garrison in Santiago de Cuba. There is now a memorial plaque on Calle Jovellar.*

★Callejón Hamel

Salvador González Art Studio, Hamel 1054 entre Aramburu y Hospital, **T** 781661, ppaula@yahoo.com *Map 3, H7, p251*
(See also p155)

Cayo Hueso has lots of little alleyways, one of which, Callejón Hamel, an extension of Calle Animas, between Aramburu and Espada, unites two art forms: music and visual arts. It is home to Salvador González Escalona's art studio. González is a self-taught painter and sculptor, inspired by the history of the neighbourhood, which is no stranger to Santería. He has painted large, bright Afro-Cuban murals on the walls of Hamel with a mixture of abstract and surrealist design. The murals also carry several phrases giving advice and warnings about danger, death and life. For example, "*¿pa'que tu me llamas, si tu no me conoces?*" (Why are you calling me, if you don't know me?), a reference to bad spirits. The community-based project, with the first open-air mural in Cuba dedicated to Santería and reflecting Afro-Cuban scenes, opened in 1990. As well as murals there are other surprises such as a typewriter pinned to the door of the gallery, painted drums and sculptures of corrugated iron and bike wheels. Each time a mural was completed a rumba party was held to honour the different orishas, called *Toque de Tambor* (playing of the drums). This tradition has been continued and every Sunday from 1200-1500 there is a free *Peña Cultural Alto Cubana, la Rumba de Cayo Hueso.* See p155. These are very popular events within the community, and outside, attracting large, enthusiastic crowds. Every month there are activities, including on the last Friday at 2000 a cultural event called *Té con* featuring poetry, theatre, painting and music.

On the third Saturday at 1000 there is a children's activity called *El Niño de Hamel*, including clowns, theatre groups and educational games. During the activity a child is chosen to represent Callejón Hamel.

This is a neighbourhood of *filín*, rumba and tango. Calle Horno was the site of the first cultural circle dedicated to Carlos Gardel (the Argentine maestro of tango), and is another centre for cultural activities. Cayo Hueso has the reputation of being a bit of a rough neighbourhood and not a tourist attraction, but it is well worth a visit for its rich cultural and historical associations. It is an easy stroll from the *Hotel Nacional*, *Habana Libre* and other nearby hotels.

● *Hamel 1108 is the home of singer-songwriter Angel Díaz, and the birthplace of the musical genre known as filín (from 'feeling').*

Iglesia del Santo Angel Custodio
Peña Pobre. Entrance also on Av de las Misiones. *Map 2, H6, p249*

The Jesuits built this church in 1672 on the slight elevation of Peña Pobre hill. The original was largely destroyed by a hurricane in 1844 and rebuilt in neo-Gothic style in 1866-71. It has white, laced towers and 10 tiny chapels, no more than kneeling places, the best of which is behind the high altar. There is some interesting stained glass depicting the *conquistadores*. During the Christmas period some impressive figures around a manger are placed at the entrance.

★ **The1930s Hotel Nacional**
*A national monument which exudes vintage glamour. With its promi-
nent position in Vedado it dominates the Malecón.*

Vedado

*Along elegant, tree-lined avenues, serene neoclassical mansions rub
shoulders with fine museums, galleries, avant-garde theatres and
concert halls. In the 1950s, American ratpackers, movie stars and
gangsters cruised and boozed the boulevards and the swanky hotels.
Nowadays, chock full of bars, both sleek and seedy, raunchy salsa
clubs and titillating cabarets, tourists are still lured to this playground
of sinful excess.*

*Vedado, with its wide, planned streets, is much easier to negotiate
than Centro and is best tackled on foot. Running northeast to southwest and infused with the salty Malecón air is **Calle 23**, or **La
Rampa**, the setting for all manner of pre-revolutionary vicissitude
and vice – now a banal jumble of airline and government offices,
seasoned with steamy nightspots, and dominated by the historic*
Hotel Habana Libre. *Crouching below, looking like an*

interplanetary spacecraft in a botanical garden, is **Coppelia**, *an ice cream parlour and post-revolutionary symbol of egalitarianism where thousands of lip-smacking Cubans queue each week for their fix of confectionary Nirvana. Calle 23 reaches the unmissable* **Cementerio Colón**, *before sweeping down to the* **Río Almendares**.

The wide, grandiose **Avenida de los Presidentes** *(G), running southeast from the Malecón, is a stellar of neoclassical, romantic and art nouveau architecture, bisected by leafy streets. Here the paradox of* habanero life *unfolds – bourgeois homes provide the backdrop to the austerity of communist subsistence. Ailing mansions slump, the gnarled roots of banyon trees rupture pavements, preened pooches strut, pink-humped* camellos *lumber past queues of locals, and 15-year-old girls,* quinceañeras, *sashay through Vedado's manicured parks, decked out like prom queens, in time-honoured celebration of their coming of age. Running parallel to Avenida de los Presidentes,* **Paseo**, *thrusts purposefully down to* **Plaza de la Revolución**. *Cold, lifeless and bleak, it is a utilitarian complex of government buildings. Still, tourists flock, rightly so, to the awesome, iconic sculptured steel monument to Che Guevara and the cool, ethereal marble statue of José Martí, but, as the site of Fidel's major speeches, it is frequently transformed into humanity en masse when half of Havana turns out for parades.*

▸▸ *See Sleeping, p116, Eating and drinking, p134, and Bars and clubs, p156 and p161.*

◉ Sights

★ **Plaza de la Revolución**
Map 3, J1, p251

Havana's political epicentre, Plaza de la Revolución, is a concrete wasteland of monoliths, incongruously clustered around the ethereal statue of José Martí. Completed just one year before the

★ Che Guevara and the Plaza de la Revolución

One of the more iconic images of the 20th century - Che Guevara, the embodiment of revolutionary ideals, sculptured in steel and suspended from the Ministry of Interior building.

Revolution, this 17-m statue of the national hero was carved from white marble extracted from La Isla de la Juventud. The base of the monument serves as a platform for Fidel to make his marathon addresses to the masses, frequently invoking the much-quoted maxims of Martí. Usually devoid of life, the plaza comes alive with patriotic zeal for the *Día de los Trabajadores* (Workers' Day). Decked out in regulation revolutionary branded t-shirts, *Habaneros* and *campesinos*, bus loaded in from the provinces, clutch Che flags, and chant nationalist slogans, in a well-orchestrated demonstration of revolutionary allegiance.

The plaza was also the site of Pope John Paul II's mass and address to the Cuban people in 1998. It is alleged Fidel cordoned off sections of the plaza to limit capacity, so as to convey the image of a half empty square, to downplay the Pope's mass appeal. The drab Soviet-style towers contain the state's institutional powerhouse, including the Presidential Palace – HQ of Fidel and the Communist Party machine, the Ministry of Communications and the Ministry of Defence building. The most arresting is the Ministry of Interior building, adorned with a steel sculpture of Che Guevara, a replica of the iconic image, originally shot in 1960, by the celebrated photographer Alberto Korda. Wearing his famous black beret, wild flowing hair and messianic stare, this potent image of Che came to represent the physical embodiment of the Cuban Revolution. The 30-metre tall steel effigy hangs from the building where Che served as minister, underneath, the motto "Hasta la Victoria Siempre" (Always, Everyday Revolution).

★ Memorial and Museo José Martí

Plaza de la Revolución, **T** 820906/840551. *Mon-Sat 0930-1730, Sun 1000-1400. US$3, lookout US$5. Map 3, J1, p251*

The marble obelisk fronted by the José Martí monument was restored in 1996 and reopened as an impressive museum. Dedicated to the life of Cuba's national hero, it provides a detailed and engaging retrospective on Martí's dramatic life, evoked through photography, letters, drawings and other artefacts. Rather less gripping are the displays recounting the tower's construction. Don't miss the lookout accessed by mirrored lift. This is the highest point in the city with good panoramic views of Havana. You should receive a certificate from the lift attendant on your descent.

Museo Postal Cubano, Ministry of Communications

Plaza de la Revolución, **T** 705193. *Mon-Fri 0900-1600. US$1. Map 3, I2, p251*

A must for dedicated philatelists, the postal museum informatively charts the history of the postal service. There is an extensive collection of Cuban stamps, including the first to be circulated in

1855, and stamps from the world over, including rare examples of the English Penny Black, dating back to 1850, and the story books of José Antonio de Armona (1765).

★ Cementerio Colón

Zapata y 12. *Rumbos* bar opposite the cemetery gates. *US$1 entrance and US$1 for good map.* Map 4, D11, p253

The Columbus Cemetery is one of Havana's must see sights. Constructed in 1871, the 56-ha city of the dead, is the second largest cemetery in the world. Soaked in myth, legend and historical significance, it contains a wealth of funerary sculpture, and its ethereal tranquillity is a heavenly relief after the utilitarianism of nearby Plaza de la Revolución. The cemetery was designed by Spanish architect Calixto de Lloira y Cardosa, who ironically became the first inhabitant of his creation, when he died at the age of 33, shortly after the project's completion. The entrance gateway, an awesome neo-Gothic representation of the Holy Trinity, leads to a grid of avenues flanked by extravagant tombs and mausoleums, and culminating in the stunning Capilla, (chapel), centrepiece. Here lie members of the sugar plantocracy and US capitalists, turning in their graves no doubt at being buried alongside revolutionary freedom fighters and literary heroes, including Máximo Gómez, Haydée Santamaría and Alejo Carpentier.

Calle 3, entre F y G Amelia de Milagrosa died in childbirth in 1901 and was buried with her baby at her side. When the body was exhumed years later, the baby was found in her arms. Each year thousands visit the grave of this legend, known as *La Milagrosa*, in search of miracles. Symbolic offerings are laid alongside the grave: baby clothes for infertility; flowers for ill health; and, bizarrely, toy cars for financial woes. Voyeuristic tour groups mix and mingle with the devout, in search of a shot rather than a miracle.

★ **Heavenly Havana**
The funerary sculptures of the ethereal Cementerio Colón.

Calle 8 entre F y G The leader of the Orthodox Party, Eduardo Chibás killed himself during a live radio broadcast in protest against the rampant corruption in Cuban politics. A shrine to revolutionary martyrdom, Chibás' grave also marks the spot where Fidel's oratory odyssey was initiated; using Chibás' grave as a platform, he delivered a fire and brimstone speech on the institutionalised evil of the establishment.

Casa de la Amistad
Paseo 406 entre 17 y 19, **T** 303114. *Map 4, C12, p253*

Dating from 1926, this elegant coral-pink renaissance-style mansion, with lush gardens and art deco interior, is now operated by ICAP (Cuban Institute for Friendship among the Peoples) and houses the *Amistur* travel agency. On the ground floor of the house

★ **Stops on the revolutionary trail**

 Best

- •Museo de la Revolución, p 59.
- •Plaza de la Revolución, p 71.
- •Castillo de Farnés, p 149.
- •Nuevo Vedado, p 117.
- •Calle Jovellar, p 68.

there is a gallery with rotating exhibits of plastic arts from Cuban and international artists. There is also a shop (0930-1800), selling antiques and reproductions, jewellery and souvenir knick-knacks. There is a reasonably priced bar with plenty of lazy day tunes courtesy of the resident quartet, and a cafeteria, where you can eat on the balcony overlooking the garden, serving consistently good food with large portions. There are two menus: one has lobster and shrimp; the other is a house menu. Indoors is the *Primavera* restaurant, elegant furniture and expensive, see Eating, p138. Dance classes can be arranged with Domingo Pau, principal dancer and choreographer with the Ballet Folklórico Nacional, priced at US$200 for a 10-day course, which includes two-three hours of classes per day and plenty of chance to practise by night.

Museo de Artes Decorativas
Calle 17 502 esquina E, **T** 308037.   *Tue-Sat 1100-1830.*
US$2. Map 3, D2, p250

Housed in a French Renaissance-style mansion since 1964, the Museum of Decorative Arts has at its disposal more than 30,000 works, including European art dating back to the reign of Louis XV, and a striking display of Oriental art spanning the 16th-20th centuries. The mansion was originally designed by Alberto Camacho (1924-27) for José Gómez Mena's daughter, from one of Cuba's wealthiest families. Most of the building materials were imported

José Martí (1853-95)

Born into a poor family in Havana, Martí dedicated his life to rebellion against Spanish rule. His headmaster, poet and freedom fighter Rafael Mendive, was a strong influence on him, and it was his connection with Mendive that was used as evidence for Martí's sentence of forced labour for his part in the 1868 Independence Conspiracy. The experience of gross injustice, slaving with old men and boys chained at the ankles, implanted in the young Martí a lifelong commitment to the struggle for independence from Spain. Martí's sentence was commuted to exile. He was sent to Spain (1871-74) where he wrote *El presidio político de Cuba*, in which he denounced the sufferings of Cubans at the hands of an authoritarian rule. He completed his studies then went to Latin America. His last years of exile were spent in the USA. He left in 1895 to join the liberation movement in Cuba, where he was welcomed as a political leader. He was killed on 19 May that year while fighting in the War of Independence. Martí's work was primarily concerned with the liberation of Cuba, but many of his poems focused on nature, with Man at the centre engaged in a process of betterment. He combined a love of poetry with a desire for his prose to have some effect on the world; his energies were directed towards securing a future in which justice and happiness could flourish. Martí set the tone for all his poetry with *Ismaelillo* (1882), demon-strating the simplicity and sincerity he felt was lacking in current Spanish poetry. He developed this style in 1878 with *Versos libres*, and later in *Versos sencillos* (1891), in which the upheavals of his own life were his biggest inspiration. He is best known in Europe by the song *Guantánamera* – an adaptation by Pete Seeger of Martí's verse, put to the melody of Joseíto Fernández. In Cuba he is the figurehead of Cuban liberation.

from France. In the 1930s the mansion was occupied by Gómez' sister, María Luisa, Condesa de Revilla de Camargo, who was a fervent collector of fine art and held elegant society dinners and receptions for guests including the Duke of Windsor and Wallace Simpson. Her valuable collections were found in the basement after the family fled Cuba following the Revolution. The interior decoration was by House of Jansen and her furniture included a desk that had belonged to Marie Antoinette.

Permanent exhibition halls with works from the 16th to 20th centuries including ceramics, porcelain (Sèvres, Chantilly and Wedgwood), furniture (Boudin, Simoneau, Chippendale and Riesener) and paintings. The Regency-inspired dining room is recommended viewing, exquisitely upholstered with Italian marble and featuring 18th-century Aubusson tapestries, Martinot clockworks, bronze candelabras and Chinese figurines. There is an extravagant collection of dinner services, including that of José Martí. The attendants are very knowledgeable and informative about the exhibits, but only in Spanish.

Parque John Lennon
Calle 17 entre 6 y 8. *Map 4, C11, p253*

The recently re-landscaped and renamed John Lennon Park\ features a bronze statue of The Beatles' singer sitting on a bench, sculpted by José Villa, who also sculpted the Che Guevara monument at the Palacio de los Pioneros in Tarará, in the Playas del Este area. Evocative words from Lennon's song *Imagine* have been translated into Spanish, "*dirás que soy un soñador, pero no soy el único*" (You may say I'm a dreamer, but I'm not the only one), and etched on the ground. It was inaugurated in December 2000, attended by Fidel Castro and Silvio Rodríguez (singer/songwriter and founder of the movement of *La Nueva Trova*). Recent theft of the statue's glasses has meant there is a 24-hour security guard and the replacement glasses have been permanently fixed in place. Classical guitar concerts are sometimes held here.

● *There is a Bobby Sands memorial in Victor Hugo park, Calle 21 entre H y I, or rather a monument to the 10 hunger strikers who died in 1981in the Maze Prison H-Block in Northern Ireland. The marble monument was inaugurated by Castro and Gerry Adams, Northern Ireland's Sinn Féin president and British MP, in December 2001.*

Museo de la Danza
Calle G (Presidentes) esquina Línea, **T** 8312198. *Tue-Sat 1100-1830. US$2, guided tour US$1.* Map 3, B3, p250

Dedicated to the rich, dramatic life of Alicia Alonso, the Museum of Dance houses an interesting array of items from the dancer's personal collection and from the Ballet Nacional de Cuba. A plethora of costumes, leotards, documents, photos, trophies and medals testify to the personal and professional accomplishments of the most influential Cuban dancer and director of all time, renowned for her superb technique, classical style, and spirit of vulnerability and defiance. The high point of the museum is the bust of Alicia, sculpted by Carlos Enríquez as a homage to Alicia for her 82nd birthday. The museum also houses an impressive collection of modern Cuban art, including works by Choco, Nelsón Domínguez, Portocarrero and Zaida del Río.

Museo Napoleónico
San Miguel 1159 esquina Ronda, **T** 791460/412. *Mon-Sat 1000-1800, Sun 0900-1230. US$3.* Map 3, F5, p250

Houses 7,000 pieces from the private collection of sugar baron, Julio Lobo: paintings and other works of art, a specialized library and a collection of weaponry. Check out the tiled fencing gallery.

Cigars

Tobacco is extremely labour intensive, and is grown and processed entirely by hand. Seedlings are transplanted in October-December from the nursery when they are 18-20 cm. After a week they are weeded; after two weeks they are earthed up to maintain humidity and to increase assimilation of nutrients. At 1.4-1.6 m, side shoots are removed, encouraging the plant to grow tall with only 6-9 pairs of leaves. Harvesting takes place in January-March when the leaves are hung on a pole to dry. The leaves turn yellow, then reddish gold and are considered dry after 50 days. They are then stacked for 30 days when fermentation takes place at a temperature not exceeding 35°C, before being classified according to colour, size and quality for wrappers or fillers. The leaves are then stripped off the main vein, dampened, flattened and packed in stacks for up to 60 days of fermentation at a temperature not exceeding 42°C. Finally they are aged for months, sometimes years, before being rolled by factory workers equipped with a *chaveta* (special knife), a guillotine and a pot of gum. A skilled *torcedor* (artisan) makes an average of 120 cigars a day as they listen to readings from the press or novels, a tradition dating from 1865. Quality control is rigid. Cigars not meeting the standards of size, shape, thickness and appearance are rejected. Those which do are stored at 16°-18°C at a humidity of 65%-70% for several weeks until they lose the moisture acquired during rolling. A specialist then classifies them according to colour (there are 65 tones) and they are chosen for boxes, with colours ranging from dark to light, left to right. They have to remain as they are placed in the box and the person who labels each cigar has to keep them in the same order, facing the same way. Finally the boxes are stamped and sealed with the guarantee: "Cuban Government's warranty for cigars exported from Havana" in Spanish, English, French and German.

Casa de las Américas

Calle G (Presidentes) esquina 5, www.casa.cult.cu *Tue-Sat 1000-1700, Sun 0900-1300. US$2. Map 3, A3, p250*

Housed in a sleek art-deco style tower fronting the Malecón, the Casa de las Américas was founded in 1959 by Haydée Santamaría for pan-American cultural promotion and interchange. This active and welcoming centre hosts a varied programme of seminars, workshops and investigative studies, in addition to running its own publishing house. Temporary exhibitions of high calibre artworks from all corners of Latin America are assembled in the Galería Latinoamericana. The Sala Contemporánea, boasts a fine ensemble of contemporary Cuban art. Renowned visiting Latino literati, including Gabriel García Márquez, have had kudos-boosting impact on this well-respected institution. On the ground floor is the Librería Rayuela book and music shop, in addition to a smaller peso bookstall. Housed next door is another Latin American artistic showcase, **Galería Haydée Santamaría**, which houses more than 6,000 works of art, representing mostly 20th-century styles including sculptures, engravings and photography exhibits. The gallery was renovated with the help of the city of Seville and reopened in 1999.

Coppelia

Calle 23 y L, opposite Hotel Habana Libre. *In theory, kiosks open 24 hrs, but in reality, Tue-Sun 1100-2230. Map 3, E5, p250*

Ice cream is the passion of the masses. The one-time pleasure preserve of the bourgeoisie, Cubans wait and salivate, on average for more than an hour, for their daily ritual. Making up for decades of deprivation, they indulge with a frenzy, shunning cones on the go in favour of dollop upon dollop of ice cream, served atop slabs of cake and drenched with sauces. A visit to *Coppelia* is a must, as much for the ice cream as for the people-watching potential.

Capitolio
The golden dome of Capitolio dominates La Habana Vieja skyline.

The parlour shot to fame as a setting for Tomás Gutiérrez Alea's 1993 seminal film *Fresa y Chocolate*. Revolutionary in design and concept, the uber-parlour, set among leafy gardens, occupies a whole block. Designed by Mario Girona in 1966, and based on an idea by Celia Sánchez Manduley, heroine of the Sierra Maestra, it exemplifies the architectural creativity of the post-Revolution years. Refurbished in 1998, it has a capacity for 707 seated ice cream lovers, see p139.

The José Martí Sports Ground
El Malecón entre Presidentes y J. *Map 3, A3, p250*

The José Martí sports ground, at the seaward end of Avenida de los Presidentes, is a good example of post-revolutionary architecture; built in 1961, it shows a highly imaginative use of concrete, painted in primary colours.

Monumento al Maine
El Malecón *Map 3, D7, p250*

Close to *Hotel Nacional*, the Monumento al Maine is a tribute to the 265 men who were killed when the *USS Maine* warship exploded in the bay in 1898. When revolutionary zeal took hold in 1959, the eagle was broken off from the top of the monument. The plaque erected by Fidel reads "To the victims of the Maine, sacrificed by imperialist greed in its determination to sieze the island of Cuba".

● *The Tribuna Anti-Imperialista José Martí built during the Elián González affair shows a statue of Martí holding his son Ismaelillo and pointing towards the US Interests Section fronted by a veil of mirrored glass windows and patrolled by Cuban military personnel. The famous billboard, with a fanatical Uncle Sam towering menacingly over a young Cuban patriot, has been relocated behind the Interests Section.*

Exploding cigars and other plots

The number of CIA-backed attempts on Castro's life is legendary. Extraordinary stories so far published include an attempt with an exploding cigar and a special powder placed in his shoes to make his beard fall out. But, failing to assassinate or maim him, the US administration in the 1960s put an extraordinary amount of effort into trying to discredit him. Many covert plans were put forward to Operation Mongoose, an anti-Castro destabilization project. One plan, Operation Dirty Trick, was to blame Castro if anything went wrong with US space flights, specifically John Glenn's flight into orbit in 1962. The Pentagon was to provide 'irrevocable proof' that if anything happened it was the fault of the Cubans and their electronic interference. Another idea was to sabotage a US plane and claim a Cuban aircraft had shot down a civilian airliner. Yet another was to sink a US warship and blame Castro.

None of these came to anything, but sabotage did take place. Cuban emigrés received help from a special CIA budget to destroy Cuba. In 1960, a French ship carrying armaments from Belgium was blown up in Havana harbour, killing 81 people and wounding hundreds. Pressure was put on British companies by the USA to stop them trading with Cuba. Having 'discouraged' British ships from transporting a cargo of British Leyland buses and spare parts, but having failed to get the deal cancelled, it was therefore more than coincidental that an East German ship carrying the equipment was rammed in the Thames. Cuba has claimed other sabotage, such as supplying asymmetrical ball bearings to damage machinery, and chemical additives in lubricants for engines to make them wear out quickly.

Miramar

Just 16 km west of the old city, but aesthetically worlds apart, Miramar has all the appearance of a wealthy suburb. Lying on the west side of the Río Almendares it is easily reached by bus, via two road tunnels or bridges. Easy on the eye, it's a relaxed strolling ground of broad avenues, lined with early 20th-century art nouveau mansions, graceful fountains and romantic parks.

While Miramar may be low on tourist magnets, it's a soothing antidote to the frenetic pace of the old town. Home to Cuba's upper crust, and banking the lion's share of the bucks sent over from the family in Miami, Miramar's leisure pursuits have a more aspirational European feel than other more gritty areas of the city. Its varied crop of restaurants and paladares are well worth shelling out the cab fare for.

While sleek, brushed steel seems the order of the day for the district's modern architectural flourishes, the nightlife remains quintessentially Havana. Raunchy discos, great, live salsa venues and flamboyant nightclubs, including the internationally renowned Tropicana cabaret show, can be found here.

▸▸ *See Eating and drinking, p141 and Bars and clubs p160.*

 Sights

Maqueta de la Ciudad

Calle 28 113 entre 1 y 3, **T** 332661/225506. *Tue-Sat 1000-1730. US$3, children US$1. Map 4, B4, p252*

Opened in 1995, this is now a great attraction and gives a good idea of the layout of Havana and its suburbs. The 88 sq m model covers Havana and its suburbs as far out as Cojímar and the airport. Colonial buildings are in red, post-colonial pre-Revolution buildings in yellow and post-Revolution buildings in white. Some of the model is difficult to see, especially in the middle, but there is an upper viewing gallery with two telescopes where it is a little easier to see. Good fun, every building is represented.

Acuario

Calle 62 y Av 3, **T** 2036401, acuario@ama.cu *Tue-Sun 1000-1800.*
Map 4, B1, p252

The national aquarium specializes in salt water fish and dolphins. It was modernized in 1999 with a new section featuring interactive sea lion and dolphin displays. Many creatures are confined to very small tanks. The **Acuario Parque Lenín** has freshwater fish.

Museums and galleries

- **Capitolio** The imposing symbol of US imperialism, but not as we know it, p64.
- **Casa de Africa** Afro-Cuban religious and cultural enlightenment, the essential stop on the Afro trail, p45.
- **Casa de Guayasimín** The life and work of one of Ecuador's most renowned artists, p45.
- **Casa de la Amistad** Colonial eye candy, rotating art exhibits, and a top musical venue, p75.
- **Casa de los Arabes** Arabic artefacts galore, featuring the only mosque in Havana, p46.
- **Casa de Simón Bolívar** The life of the iconic liberator revealed, and a varied collection of Latin-American art exhibited, p44.
- **Centro de Arte Contemporáneo Wilfredo Lam** Premier gallery exhibiting the work of home-grown and international masters, p39.
- **Castillo de la Real Fuerza and Museo de la Cerámica Cubana** This impressive fort houses ceramic art from the 1940s to the present day, p35.
- **Castillo del Morro** This colonial fortification charts Cuban history since Columbus, p41.
- **Centro de las Artes Visuales** Modern art exhibitions on a rotating basis, p52.
- **El Templete** The spot where it all began, this Doric temple houses the allegorical canvases of Jean Bautiste Vermay, p34.
- **Estudio Galería Rigoberto Mena** Abstract excellence from one of Cuba's premier contemporary artists, p43.

Museums and galleries

Listings

- **Fortaleza de San Carlos de la Cabaña** The imposing fortress where the blood of political prisoners was spilled and the revolutionary triumph of Che was celebrated, events now charted through two museums, p41.
- **Galería de Arte Carmen Montilla Tinoco** Cuban and international art and unmissable Sosabravo mural, p46.
- **Galería Los Oficios** Local artist Nelsón Dominguéz's bohemian hangout, p48.
- **La Casa Benito Juárez (Casa de México)** Beautiful house, but essentially unmaximised space, with a limited collection of Mexican arts and crafts, p47.
- **La Casa de la Obra-Pía** 18th and 19th century furnishings and a small Alejo Carpentier exhibit housed inside a colonial palace, p44.
- **Memorial and Museo José Martí** The sensational life and work of Cuba's legendary hero, p73.
- **Museo Casa Natal de José Martí** The birth place and more revelations on the great man's life, p56.
- **Museo de Arqueología** Old Town archaeological findings and aboriginal artefacts, p39.
- **Museo de Artes Decorativas** 10 exhibition halls featuring stunning furnishings and art works, spanning the 16th-20th centuries, p76.
- **Museo de la Ciudad (Palacio de los Capitanes Generales)** 19th-century portraits, military artefacts and lavish furnishings housed in this baroque palace, p35.
- **Museo de la Danza** A homage to the legendary dancer Alicia Alonso, p79.

Museums and galleries

- **Museo de Arte Colonial** Aristocratic excess revealed through an elaborate display of 17th-century furnishings, p39.
- **Museo de Automóviles** Cuba's techno-dinosaurs, displayed in all their vintage glory, p47.
- Museo de Naipes A huge collection of cards and production materials from the world over, p53.
- **Museo de la Revolución** Everything you ever wanted to know about the Revolution, p59.
- **Museo del Ron** A heady shrine to *Havana Club*, p53.
- **Museo Histórico de las Ciencias Carlos J Finlay** Cuban scientific advancements, in the name of one of the greatest Cuban doctors, p48.
- **Museo Humboldt** Botanical findings from the explorations of one of the greatest naturalists, p46.
- **Museo Nacional de Bellas Artes, Palacio de Bellas Artes** US$500 million worth of Cuban colonial and modern art, and international masterpieces, p60.
- **Museo Nacional de Historia Natural** Exhibits on the evolution of life and archaeology, and lots of stuffed animals, p36.
- **Museo Nacional de la Música** Havana's musical heritage in a nutshell, p40.
- **Museo Napoleónico** An extensive personal collection dedicated to Napoleon Bonaporte, p79.
- **Museo Numismático** The choice for dedicated numismatics, p48.
- **Museo Postal Cubano, Ministry of Communications** The development of the postal service in Cuba, including a huge stamp collection, p73.

Playas del Este 93

Tropical beaches, flanked by luscious palms leading to the aquamarine blue sea...

Cojímar 94

Literary leanings at this seaside location associated with Ernest Hemingway.

Regla   95

A stone's throw from La Habana Vieja and infused with the spirit of Santería.

Guanabacoa 95

Memorials to Holocaust victims and martyrs of the Machado dictatorship at the Jewish cemetery.

Southern Havana 96

Horse riding and boating at Parque Lenín, a wander amid the plant life at the Zen-like botanical gardens and a peek (just about) into Hemingway's finca.

Cubanacán district   98

Grandiose, isolated art schools – one with a curious female twist.

Western Havana 100

Fishy business at Marina Hemingway where the world's anglers take to the sea.

Playas del Este

Several trains depart daily from La Coubre terminal, Estación Central, Havana (40 pesos) and buses also. If you are short of time however it is best to take a taxi, US$12-15 each way, or an organized excursion, see p29 and 211. Map 1, p247 and Map 5, p254-255

This is the all-encompassing name for a truly tropical string of beaches within easy reach of Havana, which arguably surpass Varadero's brand of beach heaven. The only blot on the picture postcard landscape is the ugly concrete mass of hotels, which erupt sporadically along the coastline.

Travelling east, the first stretch is the pleasant little horseshoe beach of **Bacuranao**, 15 km from Havana and popular with locals. At the far end of the beach is a villa complex with restaurant and bar. Then comes **Tarará**, famous for its hospital where Chernobyl victims have been treated, and which also has a marina, and **El Mégano.**

Santa María del Mar is the most tourist-oriented stretch of beach. A swathe of golden sand shelves gently to vivid crystal blue waters, lined with palm trees, and dotted with tiki bars, sun loungers and an array of watersports facilities. With bronzed bodies, cooling mojitos and swinging salsa on tap, it is the hip spot to chill out, flirt and play. For more undistracted sun worship, continue further eastwards to the pretty, dune-backed **Boca Ciega** – a pleasant, non-touristy beach 27 km from Havana. At the weekend cars roll in, line up and deposit their cargo of sun worshippers at the sea's edge transforming the beach into a seething mass of baking flesh. For a more authentic seaside ambience, head to the pleasant, if rather more rough-hewn, beach of **Guanabo**. The sand is rather murky, the sea not so sparkly, and facilities are geared towards Cubans. The quietest spot is **Brisas del Mar**, at the east end. For watersports, see p191.

▶ Abakuá Secret Society

The Abakuá Secret Society is found almost exclusively in Havana (particularly in the Guanabacoa, Regla and Marianao districts), and in the cities of Matanzas, Cárdenas and Cienfuegos. It has a strong following among dock workers; indeed, outsiders often claim its members have de facto control over those ports.

As its name suggests, it is not a religion but a closed sect. Open to men only, and upholding traditional macho virtues, it has been described as an Afro-Cuban freemasonry, though it claims many non-black devotees.

Also known as *ñañiguismo*, the sect originated among slaves brought from the Calabar region of southern Nigeria and Cameroon, whose Cuban descendants are called *carabalí*. Some *ñáñigos* claim the society was formally founded in 1836 in Regla, across the bay from Havana, but there is evidence that it already existed at the time of the 1812 anti-slavery conspiracy.

Abakuá shares with freemasonry the fraternal aims of mutual assistance, as well as a series of seven secret commandments, secret signs and arcane ceremonies involving special vestments.

Cojímar

The former seaside village, 15 minutes by taxi from central Havana (*Map 1, p247*), now a concrete jungle, featured in Hemingway's *The Old Man and the Sea*, is an easy excursion. Hemingway celebrated his Nobel prize here in 1954 and there is a bust of him opposite a fort. The coastline is covered in sharp rocks and is dirty because of tanker effluent. *La Terraza* is a restaurant with photographs of Hemingway covering the walls, a pleasant view and over-priced seafood meals.

Regla

Take a ferry from near the Customs House, in La Habana Vieja, or the Ruta 6 bus from Zulueta y Virtudes inland to this eastern district. The main street, Martí, runs north from the landing stage up to the church. The museum is next to the church. US$2. Map 1, p247

Regla has a largely black population and a long, rich and still active cultural history of the Yoruba and Santería (see box, p66). The **Museo Municipal de Regla**, Martí 158 entre Facciolo y La Piedra, has an extension room with information and objects of Yoruba culture, but it is not always open. Three blocks further on is the Casa de la Cultura, which has very occasional cultural activities.

Guanabacoa

Guanabacoa is 5 km to the east of La Habana Vieja and is reached by a road turning off the Central Highway. You can take the 40-centavo bus Ruta 5 (1 hr) from 19 de Mayo, at the terminal opposite the Sala Polivalente Ramón Fonst, or by launch from Muelle Luz, at the end of Santa Clara, La Habana Vieja, to Regla, then by bus direct to Guanabacoa. Map 1, p247

Guanabacoa, a small colonial town, has an old parish church that has a splendid altar, the monastery of San Francisco, the Carral theatre and some attractive mansions. The main reason for a visit however is the **Cementerio de Judíos** (Jewish Cemetery). It was founded in 1906-10 and is set back behind an impressive gated entrance on the left on the road to Santa Fé. There is a monument to the victims of the Second World War Holocaust and bars of soap are buried as a symbolic gesture. Saúl Yelín (1935-77), one of the founding members of Cuban cinema, is buried under a large, flamboyant tree and you can also see the graves of the *Mártires del Partido Comunista*, victims of the Machado dictatorship.

Another reason to visit is for the **Museo Municipal de Guanabacoa**, Bazar de los Orishas, Martí 108 entre Versalles y San Antonio, a former estate mansion with slave quarters at the back of the building. The Festival de Raíces Africanas Wemilere is held here every November. The museum has been closed for repairs since 1999, and is scheduled to reopen in 2003. The African religion section has been transferred to Casa de Africa, see p45. However, there is a temporary Sala de Yoruba in the same street which museum staff will direct you to.

Southern Havana

Parque Lenín
Calle100 y Cortina de la Presa, Arroyo Naranjo. *South of Havana. Taxi US$15 one way, negotiable. Map 1, p247*

Northwest of Rancho Boyeros and the airport, Parque Lenín is a huge 745-ha green space on the edge of Havana, which is a popular weekend escape for Cuban families. The park is a great place to unwind from the city hubbub for a day and there is plenty of entertainment for adults and children. There is an amusement park, ampitheatre, horses for hire (see p190), outdoor cinema, boating lake, motorcross circuit, rodeo, bicycle hire, four swimming pools, art galleries, book shops, an aquarium, a range of cafés and upmarket restaurants.

A train circulates the park allowing you to get on and off at will. Pick up a map from the information centre close to the entrance. Hiring bikes has been recommended as a good way to visit; alternatively try getting on a *camello* (see Bus, p26).

Jardín Botánico Nacional de Cuba

Km 3.5, Carretera Rocío, Calabazar, south of the city beyond Parque Lenín, **T** 547278. *Mon-Sun 0900-1600. US$1, children US$0.50. A multilingual guide will meet you at the gate, no charge. Take Camello M6 and omnibus 88. Taxi from La Habana Vieja can be negotiated down to US$15 one-way, the best value if there are several of you. Many hotel tour desks offer day trips with lunch for US$25, better value than going independently and less effort. Map 1, p247*

Opened in 1984, the botanical garden is well maintained with excellent collections, including a Japanese garden with tropical adaptations. You can take a 'train' tour along the 35 km of roads around the 600-ha site, which takes about two hours. There are few signs, so it is not as informative as it might be, and a guide is helpful, describing unusual plants, which are grouped geographically in various zones. The inter-connected glass houses filled with desert, tropical and sub-tropical plants are well worth walking through.

There is a good organic vegetarian restaurant using solar energy for cooking. There is only one sitting for lunch, but you can eat as much as you like from a selection of hot and cold vegetarian dishes and drinks for US$12. Water and waste food is recycled and the restaurant grows most of its own food.

Parque Zoológico Nacional

Km 3, Carretera de Capdevilam, south Havana, **T** 447613. *Tue-Sun 0930-1530. US$3, children US$2, including tour bus trip. Taxi US$12-15. Map 1, p247*

Opened in 1984 and more akin to a safari park than a zoo, Parque Zoológico Nacional contains more than 800 animals and 100 different species sprawled across 340 ha, including elephants, giraffes, hippos, rhinos, zebras, lions and antelopes. A scientific and educational research centre, the zoo plays a large role in the preservation of endangered species. There is a reproduction area, a laboratory, clinic and a taxidermist. There is also an interactive children's area, Zoo Infantil, with smaller animals and pony rides.

Finca La Vigía

San Francisco de Paula, San Miguel del Padrón, **T** 910809. *Mon, Wed-Sat 0900-1600, Sun 0900-1230, closed Tue and on rainy days, US$5. 11 km southeast from Havana Centro. If you have time and patience, Bus P1 from Línea and P2 from 26 y 41, Vedado. Hemingway tours are offered by hotel tour desks for US$35. Map 1, p247*

Hemingway fans may wish to visit Finca La Vigía (Museo Ernest Hemingway) where he lived from 1939 to 1961. The signpost is opposite the post office. Visitors are not allowed inside the plain, whitewashed house, lovingly preserved with Hemingway's furniture, books and hunting collections, just as he left it. But you can walk all around the outside and look in through the windows and open doors, although vigilant staff prohibit any photographs unless you pay US$5 for each one. There is a small annex building with one room used for temporary exhibitions, and from the upper floors there are fine views over Havana. The tropical garden has many shady palms. Next to the empty swimming pool are the gravestones of Hemingway's pet dogs, shaded by a flowering shrub.

Cubanacán district

Architects Ricardo Porro, Roberto Gottardi and Vittorio Garati were involved in designing a revolutionary national school of art, begun in 1959. The complex was to combine schools of modern dance, plastic arts, dramatic arts, music and ballet, using domestic rather than imported materials. Deemed a "new spatial sensation", the **Escuela Superior de Arte**, Calle 120 1110 esquina 9, **T** 288075, (*Map 1, p247*) was an ambitious project of the early 1960s. Some parts were not completed and less practical schemes have been abandoned.

Hemingway's Havana

Fishing, gambling and exotic prostitutes were what attracted Ernest Hemingway to Cuba in 1932. At first he stayed at the *Hotel Ambos Mundos*. In 1940 he bought Finca La Vigía, see p98. During the Second World War, Hemingway set up his own counter-intelligence unit at the finca, calling it "the Crook Factory"; his plan was to root out Nazi spies in Havana. He also armed his fishing boat, the *Pilar*, with bazookas and hand grenades. With a crew made up of Cuban friends and Spanish exiles from the Civil War, the *Pilar* cruised the waters around Havana in search of German U-boats. The project surprisingly had the blessing of the US Embassy, who even assigned a radio operator to the *Pilar*. With no U-boats in sight for several months, the mission turned into drunken fishing trips for Hemingway, his two sons and his friends. When Hemingway returned to Cuba after more heroic contributions to the war effort in France, he wrote *The Old Man and the Sea*, the novel that won him the Nobel Prize. This was a period of particularly heavy drinking for Hemingway: early morning Scotches were followed by Papa Dobles (2½ jiggers of white rum, juice of half a grapefruit, six drops of maraschino, mixed until foaming) at the *Floridita*, absinthe in the evening, two bottles of wine with dinner, and Scotch and soda till the early hours in the casinos. When the political situation grew tense in 1958, a government patrol shot one of Hemingway's dogs. By then he was older and wearier and he went back to his Idaho home. He made a public show of his support for the Revolution on his return to Cuba. His last days at the finca were taken up with work on *The Dangerous Summer*, (on bullfighting), but his thoughts turned to suicide, and he left for Florida in 1960. After the Bay of Pigs invasion, the government appropriated the finca. Hemingway committed suicide in the USA in 1961.

You can still visit the **Escuela Superior de Artes Plásticas**, a series of interlinked pavilions, courtyards and sinuous walkways designed by Porro (which has been described as laid out in the form of a woman's body, although some see it more as the womb itself, with a cervix-like fountain in the centre).

There is also the **Escuela Superior de Artes Escénicas**, built by Gottardi, in the form of a miniature Italian hill-top town, rather claustrophobic and quite unlike Porro's sprawling, "permeable" designs, which are full of fresh air and tropical vegetation. Porro's Dance School, although part of the same complex, is not accessible via the Country Club (now the Music School, the 1960s Music School by Garati being now in ruins). Lack of maintenance, water leaks, a faulty drainage system, structural defects, vegetation and vandalism have led to deterioration of both the finished and unfinished buildings and there is a lack of funds for drawing up a master plan as well as carrying out repairs.

Western Havana

Off Av 5, 20 mins by taxi (US$10-15) from Havana.   Map 1, p247

The **Marina Hemingway** tourist complex is in the fishing village of Santa Fé. Fishing and scuba diving trips can be arranged as well as other watersports and land-based sports. The Offshore Class 1 World Championship and the Great Island speedboat Grand Prix races are held annually during the last week in April. Other tournaments held here are listed under Festivals, p175. There are 140 slips with electricity and water and space for docking 400 recreational boats. The resort includes the hotel *El Viejo y El Mar*, restaurants, bungalows and villas for rent, shopping, watersports, facilities for yachts, sports and a tourist bureau.

Havana's top hotels are more than just a place to put your head down for the night. They have provided the backdrop for revolutionary plottings, the outpouring of literary angst, and some of the hottest shows in town. During the 1950s they were a haven for US capitalists lured by rum, roulette wheels and tropical sensuality. Accommodation for your first day in a hotel should be booked in advance of travelling, as you will have to fill in an address on your tourist card. Prices given are for a double room in high season (15 December-15 March); low season prices may be about 20% lower. All hotels are owned by the government, solely or in joint ventures with foreign partners. Generally speaking, below category C you can expect old bed linen, ill-fitting sheets, peeling paintwork, crumbling tiles and indifferent service. One of the most rewarding parts of a trip is a stay in a casa particular (private house). Cubans may rent out rooms, subject to health and hygiene regulations. Taxes and licences are high. Failure to comply is punished by ruinous fines. Snooping and snitching is commonplace.

Great value, private houses offer a high standard of accommodation which surpasses state alternatives below category C. Prices are based on a double room, (it is rare to get a single person discount), and facilities usually include air conditioning and hot and cold water. Most offer, in addition, private bathrooms, TVs, and use of the kitchen. Cubans are renowned for being house proud and cleanliness is paramount. Always try to book ahead as during high season the best homes are usually full, see Language p218. Avoid using guides or even personal recommendations from other casa particular owners. They all expect US$5 commission per night, which goes on your room rate.

In La Habana Vieja there is plenty of choice of upper and mid-range hotels and a smattering of budget hotels in the colonial heart. Most casas particulares are located off the main tourist drags in southern La Habana Vieja where the authentic neighbourhood hullabaloo can be frenetic. While it may not have the cachet of more primed tourist areas, this is a great base for a raw Havana experience.

The concentration of Havana's upper-range hotels are to be found on Vedado's languid boulevards and skirting the Malecón. A medley of 1950s mafia-style monoliths, and Moorish-style palaces , which exude faded grandeur. There are a handful of mid-range hotels close to La Rampa, but no budget options. Far and away the best value are Vedado's casas particulares. These 1920s mansions and modern apartments generally offer more spacious accommodation and creature comforts than in the old town.

State accommodation in Centro is limited to a smattering of dour mid-range hotels, but there are some excellent value casas particulares. Expect that your holiday home may lurk in a rather rough-hewn street. Don't be put off, this does not reflect the accommodation standards. On the downside, you may experience irregular supplies of water and gas, and electricity shortages. Take a torch, earplugs and a philosophical attitude.

$ Sleeping codes

LL US$200+	**C** US$ 41-60
L US$151-200	**D** US$31-40
AL US$101-150	**E** US$21-30
A US$81-100	**F** US$20 and under
B US$61-80	

Price of a double room based on two people sharing

La Habana Vieja

Casas Particulares

E Casa de Eugenio y Fabio, San Ignacio 656 entre Jesús María y Merced, **T** 8629877. *Slightly off the main drag, set back one block from the port, and just around the corner from the elaborate Church of La Merced. Map 2, L6, p249* Like stumbling onto the set of the *Antiques Roadshow* Christmas Special, this professionally run casa is stuffed with antiques and bric-à-brac from yesteryear. The double bedrooms are fully equipped and spacious, but the air conditioning can be noisy and rooms looking onto the interior courtyard are not the lightest and brightest. Generally great value all round at US$25 plus US$2.50 for a hearty breakfast served in the heady baroque dining room.

E Chez Nous, Teniente Rey (Brasil) 115 entre Cuba y San Ignacio, **T** 8626287, cheznous@cemia.imf.cu *Map 2, J6, p249* This great old house, built in 1904, nestles in the heart of southern La Habana Vieja. A mellow artistic abode, laid-back and charming host Gustavo works as a radio cultural correspondent and his wife Kathy is a painter. The two spacious colonial-style rooms are fully equipped with TV, mini bar, private balcony and the quirky shared bathroom has the original 1904 shower. The spiral staircase in the leafy interior courtyard leads up to a fantastic terrace with sun loungers and great views. A double room with breakfast is US$30. Reservations essential, Gustavo is usually chock-a-block. French is spoken.

E Jesús y María, Aguacate 518 entre Sol y Muralla,**T** 8611378. *Map 2, K5, p249* A perfectly located little nook in the centre of nitty-gritty Old Havana. True to their biblical counterparts, Mary is a warm and conscientious hostess and Jesús, who is a dab hand at the old carpentry, is constantly making improvements to the self-contained apartment and fully-equipped rooms, which all have private bathrooms. There is a leafy interior courtyard that is a great place to read, chat or enjoy a rare moment of silence, and a rooftop terrace, which provides a perfect spot for taking in some rays or for enjoying some voyeuristic peeps at street life below.

E Orlando y Lisette, Aguacate 509, Apto 301, entre Sol y Muralla, **T** 8675766. *Map 2, K5, p249* Gregarious university maths professor Lisette offers the most exuberant welcome. While the house is quite small, the decent-sized light and airy double room, with private bathroom, is fully equipped; the star feature being an excellent new mattress with overhanging inflatable pink love heart. There is a great panoramic view from the terrace out towards the Malecón. The guest's bedroom has its own entrance but if you stay here you are likely to be treated as one of the family.

Hotels

LL Parque Central, Neptuno entre Prado y Zulueta, **T** 8606627-9, **F** 606630, www.goldentuliphotels.nl/gtparquecentral *Map 2, H4, p249* Despite its much-derided design, this international standard hotel offers charming and friendly service. The plush and spacious rooms have black-out curtains and soundproofed windows and the bathrooms, with separate shower rooms, are excellent. Catering largely to groups of Americans and Canadians 'on business' there are conference facilities, a fitness centre, Mediterranean and French à la carte restaurants, grand cigar lounge, swanky leafy lobby bar, and best of all, sweeping views of Havana from the pool on the top floor.

LL-L Santa Isabel, Baratillo 9 entre O'Reilly y Narciso López, Plaza de Armas, **T** 8608201, **F** 338391. *Map 6, D5, p256* Once the palace of the Santovenia counts, the Santa Isabel first opened its doors to Havana's well-heeled visitors in 1867. Exquisitely renovated a century later, and decorated with the works of some of Cuba's finest artists, this is the height of understated luxury in an unrivalled setting on Plaza de Armas. The 27 rooms, 10 of which are suites, are tasteful and well equipped. Ask for a room on the third floor with balconies overlooking the plaza. There is a lovely central patio with a fountain and greenery and a lobby bar serving great daiquiris on the terrace.

LL-A Conde de Villanueva, Mercaderes 202 entre Lamparilla y Armargura, **T** 8629293/4, **F** 8629682, hconde@villanueva.ohch.cu *Map 6, E3, p256* This small, intimate hotel, with just nine rooms, has an old gentlemen's club ambience, courtesy of the hotel's namesake, one Claudio Martínez del Pinillo, Conde de Villanueva (1789-1853), a notable personality who promoted tobacco abroad and helped to bring the railway to Cuba. This highly regarded hotel, with friendly service, is attractively upholstered in red and green with cigar themed adornments. The tastefully decorated rooms and suites are clustered around a peaceful courtyard. Amenities include cigar shop, café, bar, good restaurant.

L-A Florida, Obispo 252 esquina Cuba, **T** 8624127, **F** 8624117. *Map 6, C2, p256* Once home to sugar barons and the Cuban well-to-do, this restored 1836 mansion opened its doors as *Hotel Florida* in 1885. A cool oasis among the hustle and bustle of Calle Obispo, with a lovely courtyard setting of marble floors, statues, pillars, archways and stained glass. The 25 rooms are all plushly decorated with high ceilings. Some have colonial balconies. The elegant *Floridiana* restaurant serves good but over-priced food, and the lobby *Florida* bar, serves great daiquiris.

AL-A Sevilla, Trocadero 55 y Prado, **T** 8608560, **F** 8608582. *Map 2, H5, p249* This great art-deco building, on the edge of Old Havana, boasts an all-star line up of previous guests. Although recently restored, works continue, much to the agitation of the guests. There are 188 rooms of 1937 vintage, most have no view and very noisy a/c. The service is dismissive and lackadaisical. The star features are the lovely ceramic tiled lobby and elegant rooftop restaurant/bar with great night views over Centro and the Malecón. The standard 4-star amenities include pool, shops, sauna and massage, and tourism bureau.

AL-A Telégrafo, Prado esquina Neptuno, **T** 8611010/ 8612242, **F** 8614741. *Map 2, H4, p249* Another legendary Havana institution dating from 1860, the Telégrafo reopened at the end of 2001 with more of a contemporary spin. With 63 well-appointed, super spacious, stylish bedrooms with great high ceilings, elaborate bathrooms and soundproofing, the Telégrafo is in the prime Parque Central location. The streamlined bar and lobby area with minimalist designs and furnishings are fused with the original 19th-century colonial features. Although it lacks the fabulous 1950s aura of many of Havana's upper-crust hotels, it offers superlative service, swanky design, creature comforts and a great feeling of space.

! Al Capone once rented the entire sixth floor of the *Hotel Sevilla* and in the imagination of Graham Greene, Wormwold resided in room 516 in *Our Man in Havana*. In reality, Nicara-guan poet Ruben Darío, depressed, penniless and drinking heavily, allegedly tried to commit suicide by jumping off the balcony of room 203 in November of 1910.

AL-B Hostal del Tejadillo, Trocadero 55 y Prado, **T** 8637283, **F** 8638830. *Map 2, H5, p249* Another quaint parador-style hostel in a charming nook of La Habana Vieja. The 32 rooms, upholstered in 18th-century colonial style, with high ceilings and tall, wooden shuttered windows, are grouped around the inner courtyard. With guest house familiarity and a cosy feeling, the *Tejadillo* is much more inviting and intimate than many of its more grandiose peers. There is a lovely lobby with plants, paintings, fountains and sculptures. The satisfyingly good breakfast is served up in the lovely dining room or in the courtyard. The lively bar is a great afternoon and early evening spot, with entertaining barmen and lively tunes.

AL-B Hostal Los Frailes, Teniente Rey (Brasil) entre Mercaderes y Oficios, **T** 8629510/8629383, **F** 8629718, recepcion@habaguanex hlosfrailes.co.cu *Map 6, F3, p256* Previously the house of Marqués Pedro Pablo Duquesne IV, a captain in the French navy who came to Havana in 1793, *Los Frailes* was recently converted into a small hotel with a monasterial theme. With a gold, metallic monk hovering in the doorway, bellboys dressed in pseudo Franciscan monks' habits, classical choral music playing in the bar and the tranquil trickle of water from the well in the lush courtyard, *Los Frailes* is an ethereal out-of-Havana experience. There are 22 rooms with a/c, phone, satellite TV, minibar and, although they don't have interior windows, they overlook the central courtyard.The 4 suites have balconies out on to the street. All meals are served at *La Marina* restaurant, 10 m from the hotel.

AL-B Inglaterra, Prado 416 entre San Rafael y San Miguel, **T** 8608595/7, **F** 8608254. *Map 2, H4, p249* Built in 1875, next to the Teatro Nacional, famous former foreign guests included Sarah Bernhardt in 1887, Gen Antonio Maceo (one of the heroes of the Cuban Wars of Independence) in 1890, and the authors Federico García Lorca and Rubén Darío in 1910. Oozing faded grandeur, the 86 colonial-style rooms can be a bit rough around the edges. With

▶ Our Man in Havana

Graham Greene's first visit to Cuba was in 1957 to research his book *Our Man in Havana*. He was originally going to set it in Lisbon, but decided on a more exotic location; he planned to sell the film rights to the novel before it was even written. He immediately took a liking to the unlimited decadence Havana had to offer, and spent much of his time at the Shanghai Theatre, a club which featured live sex shows.

Greene's former connections with the British Secret Intelligence Service gave him access to political society. He based some of the characters on Batista's soldiers: Captain Segura, with his cigarette case made of human skin, was based on the real-life Capitán Ventura. The plot of the novel involves a vacuum cleaner salesman being mistaken for a secret agent, who for fear of being discovered as a fraud, tries to carry out the orders given to him by providing diagrams of vacuum cleaner parts, pretending they are in fact the plans for an arsenal of nuclear weapons.

Greene's training as a secret agent allowed him to infiltrate all levels of political life: he made contact with Castro's rebel forces in the Sierra Maestra, offering them any help they needed. He was asked to smuggle a suitcase of warm clothes through customs on a Havana-Santiago flight, to help them survive the freezing night-time temperatures of the mountains.

In 1959, when Greene arrived for the second time in Havana to assist director Carol Reed in the filming of his novel, the Revolution had already triumphed. Greene's small act of support in 1957 had not been forgotten, and Castro gave his personal seal of approval to the film, although he felt it didn't capture the full extent of Batista's evil.

noisy a/c, and balconies overlooking Parque Central or the Cabaret Nacional, earplugs are recommended. Ask for a room overlooking the theatre where you can enjoy the early morning rehearsals of the national ballet. Some single rooms have no windows.

The elaborate, Moorish-tiled dining room is a great place to start the day, with the breakfast buffet serving up a weird spread of sticky pastries, hard rolls and fishy concoctions, redeemed by a decent selection of tropical fruit. Delightful, glazed tile pictures by famous and not-so-famous Cuban artists have been set into the pavement in front of the hotel.

A **Hotel Armadores de Santander**, Luz 4 esquina San Pedro, **T** 8628000, **F** 8628080. *Located just by the port in southern La Habana Vieja.* Map 6, H4, p256 Opened at the beginning of 2002, this 4-star-plus, nautically themed hotel has smart, gentlemanly rooms, which are well equipped with QE2-style bathrooms. Most rooms have huge, deck-style terraces – the biggest in the city – with potted plants, great views and garden furniture. Watch you don't draw the short straw on the eight interior cabins. There are smoker's lounges on each floor, a mezzanine level games room, and the welcoming bar serves great daiquiris and snacks. Making a huge effort to stamp its mark and a personality, the services are impeccable and facilities excellent value for money.

A-C **Hostal Valencia**, Oficios 53 esquina Obrapía, **T** 8671037/ 8616423, **F** 8605628, reserva@habaguanexhvalencia.co.cu Map 6, E4, p256 Originally an 18th-century private house, the tastefully restored hostal is a joint Spanish/Cuban venture mod- elled on the Spanish paradores. The rustic suites and rooms, some in better shape than others, are named after Valencian towns. Breakfast is served in the romantic courtyard setting with tweety birds and lavish cascading vines. There is an excellent restaurant *La Paella*, see p129, and bar, *Nostalgia*, see p148. Built over an archaeological site, the more discreet *Hostal El Comendador*, next door, is separate but uses the *Valencia*'s facilities. Opened in 1999, it is a peaceful, intimate and breezy hotel set over two floors, nicely decorated with great colonial bathtubs. Ask for a room overlooking the Princess Diana garden, and avoid rooms over the kitchen, which can be noisy.

A-B Plaza, Zulueta 267 esquina Neptuno, or Ignacio Agramonte 267, **T** 8608583/9, **F** 8608869. *Map 2, H4, p249* Hard to justify the 4-star category of the *Plaza*, which offers 186 generally grotty, noisy rooms with tepid water, and substandard service. If you are stuck for a bed for the night, there is usually, not surprisingly, availability at the *Plaza*. For peace and quiet, if nothing else, ask for a room in the inner courtyard. There is a poor quality breakfast, served on the 5th floor, you may have to wait 10 minutes for service, but you can enjoy a great view of Old Havana while you wait. Lots of tourist agencies put the *Plaza*'s name down on tourist cards but it's advisable to organize an alternative.

B Hostal San Miguel, Cuba 52 esquina Peña Pobre, **T** 8627656, **F** 8634088, www.hostalsanmiguel.cu *Map 2, G7, p249* Set in a great location, close to La Punta and overlooking the bay, this elegant building was once home to Antonio San Miguel y Segalá, director of *La Lucha* newspaper. An intimate hotel, with just 10 rooms, its exquisite decor reflects 1920s *habanero* bourgeois tastes and tendencies. The swanky lobby, with intricate stained glass, marble floors, chandeliers and antique furnishings, also displays the works of Cuban artists. There are fantastic views of La Punta and the Castillo de Morro from the rooftop terrace, which also serves great industrial strength cocktails and hearty breakfasts.

D-E Residencia Santa Clara, entrance on Sol y Cuba, **T** 863335, **F** 335696, reaca@cencrem.cult.cu *Map 6, G1, p256* Great value accommodation in charmingly restored colonial convent building dating from 1644. Soothing, friendly atmosphere and immaculately maintained rooms in a peaceful, laid back setting. Accommodation ranges from spacious suites with colonial furnishings to small, but perfectly formed, single rooms, to dorm-style set-ups. Don't rely on the standard, unimaginative breakfast to keep you going for the day. Group discounts available for students and tour groups.

Centro

Casas Particulares

E Carlos Luis Valderrama Moré, Neptuno 404 entre San Nicolás y Manrique, Piso 2, **T** 8679842. *Map 2, G2, p249* Situated on one of the main shopping streets in Centro, this is perfect for experiencing the authentic barrio feel of Havana away from the tourist routes of La Habana Vieja, but not so perfect if you are noise sensitive. There are two rooms: the one with the double bed is quieter but interior; the noisy twin has a great terrace, which backs onto dwellings, home to animated *habaneros*. The small twin beds are not great if you are built like Magic Johnson. Vivián and her family are very accommodating and have been making gradual renovations to the house, so call ahead to check status and availability.

E Casa Marta, Manrique 362 entre San Miguel y San Rafael, **T** 8633078. *Map 2, H2, p249* Seek among the piles of rubble in Centro Habana and ye shall find… a fluorescent, kitsch pink love heart signposting the *Casa Marta* and your charismatic host, the ex-revolutionary fighter Nelsón. With an inviting family atmosphere and communal 'hangout' courtyard, where Nelsón shares his tales of the Sierra Maestra, this European-style hostel-cum-casa is popular with long-stay guests. There are four comfortable rooms, three with shared bath and one with its own en suite facilities. Although the neighbourhood looks rather like war-torn Sarajevo, this tranquil *casa* is in a good central location, close to the Chinese market and just a 10-min walk from the entertainment and transport hub of Parque Central.

E Hostal Numática, Consulado 223 entre Animas y Trocadero, **T** 8627629. *Well connected, in an earthy Centro street, just off El Prado, it is just a five-min walk from Parque Central and the attractions and nightlife of La Habana Vieja. Map 2, G4, p249* A bit of La Pampa in Havana at this Argentine-themed casa-cum-hostel-cum-parador. The modern, tastefully designed double and twin bedrooms, with private bathrooms, mini bar, fans, a/c and TV are excellent value. Breakfast is served on request in the guests' reception room and included in the US$30 room rate. On the downside this is a more anonymous set-up and not quite the culturally rewarding casa particular experience.

E Jesús Deiro Rana, San Rafael 312 1 entre Galiano y San Nicolás, **T** 8638452. *Map 2, H2, p249* Another Aladdin's cave of colonial treasures lurking on one of the rubble-strewn arteries of central Havana. Spacious and decorative with high ceilings, leafy tiled courtyard, an amazing display of antique clocks and furnishings, including a haughty 1870 colonial bed to sleep in. The two double bedrooms are spacious and well equipped with a modern shared bathroom.

E Marilys Herrera González, Concordia 714 altos entre Soledad y Aramburo, **T** 700608, www.casaparticular.tripod.com *Map 3, G8, p251* Sandwiched between Centro Habana, Vedado and the Malecón, close to the artistic community of Cayo Hueso, this lovely house gets top marks for family atmosphere, surgical cleanliness and free flowing *Havana Club*. In addition to the two, light and airy rooms, there is also a recently refurbished apartment, fully equipped with kitchen, dining room and rooftop terrace with great views over Capitolio, La Habana Vieja and the Malecón coastline. A great choice if you want to feel like one of the family.

E **Rosa Artiles Hernández**, Crespo 117 bajos entre Colón y Trocadero, **T** 8627574. *Map 2, G4, p249* Plenty of eye candy in the form of the immaculately maintained 1950s Chevy, which occupies pride of place in this charming household. The peaceful, simple, clean rooms are well equipped, and the atmosphere is warm, caring and laid back. Close to the Malecón, and a 10-min walk from the buzz of Parque Central, this a good spot for discovering and even falling into – watch out for the pot holes late at night – the less well-trodden streets of Centro. The choice for old car aficionados. A snip at US$20.

E **Villa Colonial Tomy**, Gervasio 218, entre Virtudes y Concordia, **T** 8623125. *Map 2, F1, p248* With fingernails to rival Flo Jo and more gold than Mr T, ballet teacher Tomy is as hard to miss as his colourful home. Tomy's showcase of antiques and memorabilia include an English tea cup gallery, Spanish thrones, Italian harlequin masks, Japanese screens and photos of Tomy's former pupil Carlos Acosta, who has pirouetted himself from the Cuban to the London School of Ballet. Each bedroom is artfully decorated. While the yellow room sports the best bed, the white room houses a collection of antique swords and jewellery boxes. There is a great rooftop terrace with colourfully painted murals dedicated to Oscar Wilde. On the downside, the rooms, which lead off the interior courtyard, can be quite stuffy and the small bathroom is shared between guests, hosts and the stream of visitors.

F **Dr Alejandro Oses**, Malecón 163, p1, entre Aguilá y Crespo, **T** 8637359 *Map 2, F4, p248* For the best views in the city of the Malecón stretching from El Morro to Hotel Nacional. Although the bedrooms are interior and can be stuffy, they are clean and comfortable, and the breezy living area, setting and family atmosphere more than compensates. You can arrange dance classes with Orestes Dickinson who whips up the bountiful breakfast each morning. Don't let the less than wholesome aromas on the apartment block's communal stairway be a put off, at just US$20 per night this is a bargain and always gets booked up well in advance.

Hotels

C Caribbean, Paseo Martí (Prado) 164 esquina Colón, **T** 8608210/8608233, **F** 8609479. *Map 2, G5, p249* About as Caribbean as Skegness. The welcoming lobby defies the soulless breeze-block-style bedrooms, 36 allegedly 'remodelled' with fan and TV. Only seven of the rooms have windows, the rooms at the front are noisy, and those on the lower floors at the back are over a deafening water pump. The bonus is the location. The rooms on the 5th floor are your best bet. For all its faults, it's popular with budget travellers and the *Café del Prado* downstairs is handy for US$3 pasta, pizza and paninis from 1200-2400.

C-D La Casa del Científico, Prado 212 esquina Trocadero, **T** 8638103/8633591, **F** 8600167. *Map 2, G5, p249* This stunning, eclectic colonial building is well preserved rather than renovated. The original features are incredible, with extravagant baroque ceilings and a luxurious classic-style dining room despite the incongruous plastic garden furniture – money for refurbishment is apparently too tight too mention! The atmosphere is charmingly oldey worldey and the staff are friendly and knowledgeable. The bedrooms vary considerably in standard and facilities; it's worth checking out the available options before you commit. Floor by floor renovation work means limited availability, and reservations during high season are essential. *Asistur* office on site. One of the best state budget options on the edge of La Habana Vieja.

D   Lido, Consulado 210 entre Animas y Trocadero, **T** 8671102, **F** 338814. *Map 2, G4, p249*   On the plus side, the *Lido* is centrally located just one block from Prado, and there is a friendly reception area, with internet access, and a roof terrace bar/café. On the down side, the rooms are bleak and cell-like – few have windows and most have paint peeling off the walls and stained concrete floors. There's no hot water and the laundry service, done by hand and per item, is a total rip off. Cheap but definitely not cheerful.

Vedado

Casas Particulares

E   Adita, 9 257 entre J y I, **T** 8320643. *Map 3, B4, p250*   The dilapidated eyesore of a building and yapping hounds congregating outside belie the quirky charm of Adita's casa particular. Spanking clean with an antiques collection Sotheby's would be proud of, this is a great place to call home. The two spacious double rooms, with a smattering of religious artefacts, are fully equipped and each has its own bathroom. The house's most interesting feature is the secret passageway that leads to a self-contained apartment, with a lovely light and bedroom, bathroom, dining room and a small kitchen. At just US$20 for the double rooms and US$25 for the apartment, this is one of the best-value homes in Vedado.

E   Armando Gutiérrez, 21 62 entre M y N, Apto 7, Piso 4, **T/F** 8321876. *Map 3, D6, p250*   Close to the *Hotel Nacional*, this modern imposing block is in a great location close to the nightlife and eateries of Vedado. If privacy is what you are after, the two, tastefully designed double rooms are separated from the rest of the house and have their own entrance. Self-proclaimed historical and cultural experts, the quirky trio of Armando, his wife Betty and mother Teresa will provide you with their own local cultural titbits.

E Casa Blanca, 13 917 entre 6 y 8, **T** 8335697, www.caspar.net/casa/ *Map 4, B11, p253* The 'White House' is definitely the place to live it up in pre-revolutionary aristocratic splendour. Once home to counts and consulates this sumptuous house with marble staircases, priceless antiques and family heirlooms is run more like a quaint English B&B. True to his heritage, host Jorge is cultured, well travelled, speaks fluent English and is a great source of local information. All rooms are fully-equipped and even include their own 'salon', terrace and parking. A great central location in leafy Vedado.

E Daysie Recio, B 403 entre 17 y 19, **T** 8305609. *Map 3, D1, p250* First impressions are definitely deceptive where Casa Daysie is concerned. While the exterior of the building and communal areas of the casa may be a little rough around the edges, the guest accommodation is clean, light, airy and spacious, and Daysie is a vivacious and hospitable hostess. The accommodation is perfect for families or groups of friends, comprising two bedrooms sleeping three with an interconnecting bathroom. One of the bedrooms has a terrace overlooking a leafy backyard.

E Jorge Coallo Potts, L 456 Apto 11 entre 21 y 23. **T** 8329032. *Map 3, D5, p250* A warm, welcoming home perfectly situated in the peaceful streets of Vedado. Easy to find, temptingly close to *Coppelia*, and a stone's throw from the nightlife of La Rampa, this is a convenient base. The spacious double bedroom with private bathroom is very comfortable. Generous spirited, Jorge and Marilys are great conversationalists and a stay in their home would enrich anyone's visit to Cuba.

E Vedado Havana, Paseo 313 Apto 43 esquina 15, **T** 8334174. *Map 4, B12, p253* The shabby exterior of this modern Soviet-style apartment block belies the warm and comfortable ambience of this casa particular. A very professional set up, the accommodation comprises a tasteful double room, US$30, which is fully equipped with its own private bathroom, and a smaller room, US$20, with futon and shower room. The star quality is undoubtedly its hosts Raúl and Magaly. Revolutionary zealot Raúl will entertain and inform for hours with his press cuttings testifying to his student days as a Cuban dissident in the USA, while photos of the one-time Lieutenant Colonel who fought alongside Fidel in the Sierra Maestra, adorn the walls. For lovers of revolutionary tales, this is the definitely the pick of the bunch.

E   **Villa Babi**, 27 965 entre 6 y 8, **T** 8306373, jlrc@informed.sld.cu *Map 4, D12, p253*   A must for Cuban film buffs. This bohemian hangout, close to Cementerio Colón, is home to María del Carmen Díaz, second wife of the late Tomás Gutiérrez Alea, famed director of *Fresa y Chocolate*. A cinematic shrine, the walls are covered with María's personal collection of film memorabilia including priceless black and white images of Tomás and a glamorous young María. The welcoming ambience and literary graffiti decor more than compensates for the lack of plush fixtures and fittings. This is the best value in Vedado at US$20 and is very popular with Italians, so call ahead for reservations. María also serves bargain-priced traditional paladar cooking, including set menus for less than US$7.

E   **Apartments 18 and 19**, 25 359 entre L y K. *Centrally located across the road from the* Hotel Habana Libre. *Map 3, E5, p250*   If you haven't made a reservation, this modern, easy to find apartment block is the best spot to chance your luck. Although this 1950s building is lacking in character its inhabitants certainly are not, with a medley of bohemian *habaneros* in residence.

   Apto 18, T 8324214, run by actress María, is a laidback luvvie heaven with smock-clad María floating around the light and spacious apartment, refreshingly ventilated by the salty Malecón air. The double rooms, both with modern private bathrooms, are comfortable and spacious and have great views over Vedado. There is plenty of room for negotiation on long-term stays.

Apto 19, T 8326471, provides a great base for experiencing Havana's hedonistic pleasures. Charming and salsa-crazy Lissette will provide the scoop on the top nights out. The large double bedroom gets 10 points for the biggest and most luxurious en-suite bathroom in Havana, and for the most stylish, eclectic decor. There is a rooftop terrace with great views and a peaceful retreat from the rather yappy dog.

Hotels

LL-L Meliá Cohiba, Paseo entre 1 y 3, **T** 8333636, **F** 334555, www. solmeliacuba.com *Map 4, A12, p253* Exclusive, modern, stylish and mechanically efficient, with all the intimacy and character of an airport departure lounge. Cultivating an air of anonymity, it's a good place to go smoothly about your business unnoticed and revel in the 5 star standards, luxury and creature comforts you would expect of any international deluxe hotel: 342 rooms, 120 suites, shops, gym, healthclub, pool, gourmet restaurant, piano bar.

LL-AL Nacional de Cuba, O esquina 21, **T** 333564-7, **F** 335054/5. *Map 3, D7, p250* Dating from the 1930s, the palatial *Nacional* is a national monument, and as much a part of Havana's history as any museum. With its Beverly Hills-style driveway, sumptuous reception hall, dripping in gold and marble, and fabulous 1950s aura, the *Nacional* exudes vintage glamour, albeit a little faded. The setting is unsurpassed, and the terrace bar, with sweeping views over the Malecón, is unmissable for a cocktail at least. There are 457 rooms, some plushly renovated, some not, and swanky bathrooms with goodies galore. In the 1930s-1950s, the *Nacional* played host to the kings and queens of cool, revolutionaries and mobsters. Frank Sinatra sang at the *Paradiso Nightclub*, and nowadays celebs major and minor still flock. You

Sleeping

know you have arrived if you are put on the 8th 'Rockerfeller' floor, rubbing shoulders with the global glitterati, including Kate Moss, Matt Dillon and Naomi Campbell. Fantastic breakfasts with fruits galore, made to order omelettes, cakes, pastries and the full gamut of Cuban meat and fishy concoctions. All the amenities you would expect including steam room, two pools, restaurants, bars, shops, business centre on lobby, exchange bureau.

L Sol Meliá Tryp Habana Libre, L y 23, **T** 554011, **F** 553141, www.solmeliacuba .com *Map 3, E5, p250* Inaugurated on 19 March 1958, the *Habana Libre*, in its former guise as The Hilton, was the epitome of luxury and decadence. The hotel was a magnet for the crème de la crème of big spenders, that was until Castro and his comrades rolled in on 8 January 1959 and made room 2324 their Revolution Headquarters. Its iconic status aside, you are not likely to be bowled over by the rather anonymous, business-like atmosphere, and 606 functional, albeit remodelled, rooms. The amenities are 5-star with a swimming pool, smart restaurants, a handy cafeteria, *La Rampa*, see p138, for cheap munchies, 24-hour coffee shop, and the nightclub *Cabaret Turquino*, open 2200-0400. The shopping mall in the lobby includes *Banco Financiero Internacional*, a postal service and airline offices.

AL-B Presidente, Calzada y G, **T** 551801/4, **F** 333753. *Map 3, B3, p250* With a heady, smoky atmosphere and Italian accents and attitude, the *Presidente* has a distinctly Mafiosa edge. Located in one of the loveliest areas of Vedado, with the full range of 4-star services, including a great pool area with bar. The small but sumptuous lobby is chock full of early 20th-century furnishings, relieved by the rampant and unruly tropical plants. The oldest hotel in Havana, with 162 restored rooms – ask for a room on the 10th floor (the Colonial Floor) which has the best collection of antiques – 10 suites, and three rooms, which are fully adapted for disabled people.

▶ **Ernesto 'Che' Guevara: rise and fall of the 'New Man'**

Beginning with the triumph of the Revolution on 1 January 1959, Cubans rallied to Guevara, the ascetic outsider with a dramatic appearance and an unfamiliar accent. Nicknamed 'Che' after an Argentine figure of speech, Guevara was seen as the Revolution's second leader.

A charismatic orator, Guevara appealed to the idealism of the young, calling for the birth of a 'New Man', or a revolutionary society based on moral, rather than material incentives. His eloquence on behalf of the poor and dispossessed made him a global spokesman for the Third World, but it proved easier to be against what Che was against than for what he was for.

Once in power, Guevara endorsed show trials and summary executions of opponents and later, as head of the Central Bank and Ministry of Industry, his socialist economic reforms produced chaos even by his own account.

Frustrated by Castro's increasing reliance on the Soviet Union, Guevara quit Cuba in 1965, first to join a doomed rebellion in the Congo, then, in late 1966, to launch his own guerrilla column in Bolivia.

On 8 October 1967, in an operation co-ordinated by the CIA, Guevara was captured and executed by Bolivian troops. His remains were repatriated to Cuba 30 years later, and are now interred in a mausoleum in Santa Clara.

Guevara remains an enigmatic figure, seen as both an inspiring idealist and an inflexible ideologue. Despite his position as the Revolution's greatest hero, 'El Che' has also become a symbol of dissent for those Cubans who recall his energy and optimism at a time when the Cuban Revolution seems to lack both.

AL Victoria, 19 y M, **T** 333510/326531, **F** 333109, reserva@
gcvictoria.gca.cma.net *Map 3, D6, p250* There is a subtle elegance
and literary feel to this unassuming 4-star hotel, whose star guest
was appropriately Spanish Nobel prize-winning author Juan
Ramón Jiménez. Centrally located, the 31 rooms, are small and
tasteful, if conservative, with well-equipped bathrooms.
There is a small pool, parking and free internet access for guests.

A Habana Riviera, Paseo y Malecón, **T** 334051/5,
F 333739. *Map 4, A12, p253* Built in the 1950s, this Soviet-style
block was a symbol of pre-revolutionary hedonism. During its
heyday of sin it was the turf of mobsters Meyer Lanksy and Lucky
Luciano, who, in cahoots with the Hollywood glitterati, used it as
the base for their underworld exploits and decadent pursuits.
Tatty, rough around the edges, and pretty unfriendly to say the
least, the glamour may have faded but the decadence still remains.
The bar and *Copacabana Club* are popular pick-up joints, and the
desolate square outside is awash with prostitutes after dark – if
they haven't made it into the club inside. On the plus side, the
location is fantastic – alongside the Malecón, the rooms are
spacious and well maintained, and there is a great pool. The
cheaper end of this price bracket – for a reason.

B Vedado, O 244 entre 23 (Humboldt) y 25, **T** 334072, **F** 334186,
Hotelvedado@hotmail.com *Map 3, E6, p250* A great location,
smack bang in the heart of Vedado, with an above average range
of facilities for its 3-star rating. Renovated in 1999, the rather basic
194 rooms have satellite TV, a/c, and decent enough bathrooms.
Amenities include a concrete pool area, a Spanish and
international restaurant, gymnasium/health centre with US$10
massages, nightclub 2230-1600, admission US$10 then open bar.

Eating and drinking

Cuba certainly isn't renowned for being a foodie's paradise. Given the food shortages, it's not surprising Havana lacks the culinary credentials of Paris or Naples. Cuban chefs have traditionally served up a limited repertoire of bland meals featuring fibrous hunks of pork and chicken. But globe-trotting gourmets needn't retreat in Michelin haste – the quality of food and the dining experience seems to be on the up with beef and seafood being added to the platter.

State-owned restaurants are recognizable by the credit card stickers on the door. Generally far from gastronomic excellence, what you pay for is the setting, whether it be a Hemingway haunt, the site of a revolutionary plotting, or simply for its views. The national dish is *congrís* (rice with black beans), roast pork and yuca (cassava) or fried plantain. You can find dishes masquerading as Italian, Spanish, French and Chinese, and regardless of the price you should be prepared for a limited availability of ingredients served by disinterested staff.

Eating codes

$$$ US$30 and over

$$ US$20-30

$ US$10-20

Prices refer to the cost of a two course meal with a beer for one person.

Vegetarians in Cuba have always had a raw deal, as food is often cooked with meat or in animal fat, but an array of vegetarian restaurants have opened serving an aspiring line up of leafy greens and free-radical mopping fodder.

The paladar system, whereby Cubans invite paying guests into their homes, represents one of few private enterprise initiatives. Paladares are licensed and taxed, limited to 12 chairs and serve up delightful deviations from the traditional fodder bemoaned by travellers. Paladares are not allowed to serve lobster or shrimp, however if you ask, there are often items available. They will also serve pasta, omelettes and salads, but you are advised to book ahead with special requests. Most paladar owners serve local beer, soft drinks and coffee, along with a more enticing repertoire of industrial-strength cocktails. When a bottle of *Havana Club* costs less than US$5 in the supermarket, this is where paladar owners can really inflate their margins; blasting the tourist budget as well as the brain cells.

With a rigorous selection process, paladar dining can be one of the most culturally enriching experiences of any trip. Where else in the world can you dine in the home of a revolutionary who fought alongside Fidel? Enjoy an after dinner liqueur with one of Cuba's most renowned contemporary painters or smoke a *cohiba* with a member of the Cuban National Ballet? All for less than a fistful of dollars! Always try to use the recommendations in this guide; *jineteros* will expect a commission, so you will end up paying more.

La Habana Vieja

Paladares

$$ Don Lorenzo, Acosta 260 A entre Habana y Compostela, **T** 8616733. *1200-2400. Map 2, L5, p249* With a feisty looking German Shepherd keeping watch from the rooftop, and the local domino players keeping tracks on the street, Don is clearly king on his block. Serving the widest menu – over 50 dishes, it does beg the question what's the speciality? Crocodile – stewed, quilted and stuffed, fish, chicken, pork and lamb, served up in almond sauces, Basque style, French style, cider smothered and with the odd peachy, fruity twist to name but a few. This is a great choice for veggies with set menus for US$12.00. Fish and meat dishes are considerably more expensive than average paladares at US$15-18, but still, a great entertaining night when it's full.

$ Doña Blanquita, Prado 158 entre Colón y Refugio. *Map 2, G5, p249* When she isn't off on her jollys in Miami, the Doña runs a tight ship applying rigorous quality control to each no nonsense, traditional *comida criolla* dish. The repertoire of pork, chicken and fish are dished up with dollops of rice and beans, a token salad and with enough oil and grease to keep a 1940s Chevy running for months – be sure to specify your own *gusto*, see Food Glossary, p218, if your Spanish falters. The high priestess of kitsch, the Doña has been making renovation to her Prado palace, so call ahead to check status and availability.

$ La Moneda Cubana, San Ignacio 77 entre O'Reilly y Pedrado, **T** 8763852. *1200-2230. Map 6, B3, p256* This closet-sized paladar benefits from being in a prime location, a stone's throw from the cathedral. The four set menus of traditional Cuban fodder, including chicken, pork, fish and an omelette for vegetarians, are served with rice, beans, bananas and bread, and would definitely benefit from a touch of creative vigour. But, the decor, made up of wall-to-wall currency from all corners of the globe, and the business cards of previous diners, gives an added novelty value.

State restaurants

$$$ **El Floridita**, Obispo esquina Monserrate, next to the Parque Central, **T** 8631060. *1130-2400. Map 2, I5, p249* A favourite haunt of Hemingway, the *Floridita* is a very elegant bar and restaurant reflected in the prices (US$6 for a daiquiri). It's well worth a visit to see the sumptuous decor and 'Bogart atmosphere', but the food is poor and overpriced.

$$$ **El Patio**, San Ignacio 54 esquina Empedrado, Plaza Catedral, **T** 8618504. *24 hours. Map 6, B3, p256* While the location along-side the beautiful cathedral is sublime, the cooking remains firmly in the realm of earthy Cuban *comida*, including a selection of stodgy national dishes further weighed down by hefty price tags. The service is slapdash, but amiable, but it's not a setting you would want to be torpedoed out from at any rate.

$$$ **La Bodeguita del Medio**, Empedrado 207 entre Cuba y San Ignacio, near the cathedral, **T** 8671374 *1000-1200. Map 6, B3, p256* Tourists flock to this, the most famous Hemingway haunt of them all. A ritual shared by visiting celebs major and minor, Naomi Campbell and Matt Dillon have left their designer scrawls on the walls. It should be visited for a mojito at least, but the food is poor – avoid the greasy roast pork speciality left waiting for the next tour group influx, and expensive at US$35-40 for two.

$$ **A Prado y Neptuno**, address of the same name, opposite *Hotel Parque Central. 1200-2300. Map 2, H4, p249* Very *TGI Fridays* with video screens, fluorescent lighting, a yankee-themed bar area,

and Warholesque artwork with a revolutionary spin. Very popular with nostalgic ex-pats, escorts, locals and tourists. Substantial, reasonably-priced pasta dishes, averaging US$6, include a very tasty seafood spaghetti with lashings of mussels, prawns and squid, a rather gooey four cheese pasta, an interesting take on a mushroom risotto, chicken breast with mushrooms, and red snapper. Flecks of parmesan will cost you US$2. Good people-watching potential with window seating overlooking Parque Central.

$$ Don Giovanni, Tacón entre Empedrado y O'Reilly, **T** 8671036. *1200-2300. Map 6, C4, p256* Serene venue, shame about the Italian food. On the plus side this is a lovely, colonial building with ice-blue shutters opening out onto the bay, marble floors, chandeliers, pillars and palms, and a strangely protruding tree. It makes for a nice date setting with tables for two on the balconies, overlooking the fort, and the menu caters well for vegetarians; the D'Giovanni signature tomato and mushroom penne is the best bet. The food is generally disappointing with overpriced bland pasta dishes starting at US$5.50, often served up cold with unsatisfying small portions. Outside, from 2300 every night, except Wednesday, there is live salsa music.

$$ Dominica, O'Reilly esquina Mercaderes, **T** 8662917. *1200-2400. Map 6, C4, p256* Stick to pizza and pasta and *Dominica* is great value for money; wander off into the realms of three-course à la carte and it could soon cost you an arm, a leg and a whole torso. This is definitely the top spot in Havana for authentic, Italian oven-baked pizzas in a smart, minimalist setting, in a prime location. Choose from a range of well-topped pizzas, US$4.50-12, the large ones are big enough for two to share; or well-prepared pasta dishes, from US$6, including a spicy, substantial Arrabiata liberally endowed with anchovies, olives, chillies and fresh parmesan. The pleasant outside seating area with serenading musicians makes for a highly civilized lunch or dinner.

$$ **La Mina**, Obispo esquina Oficios, Plaza de Armas, **T** 8620216. *1200-2400. Map 6, D5, p256* Not surprisingly *La Mina* is a tourist magnet and a must on every tour group's agenda. The expensive menu is comprised of traditional, hearty Cuban staples, pretty well represented by the laminate menus. With outside seating on Plaza de Armas, and a beautiful, interior courtyard, what you are paying for is the location, people-watching potential, and buoyant atmosphere courtesy of the round-the-clock quartet. *La Mina*'s ice cream parlour around the corner on Calle Oficios is a cooling stop-off point for a US$0.50 cone.

$$ **La Paella**, *Hostal Valencia*, Oficios 53, **T** 8671037. *1200-2300. Map 6, E4, p256* The much-lauded paella is worthy of its acclaimed status as the best in Havana, but it has to be said the competition is pretty non-existent. The traditional taberna-style design with snug, wooden panelling and tastefully themed Spanish props creates a warm, inviting ambience. The service is charming and conscientious. Unfortunately the paella for two rules out those dining solo.

$$ **La Zaragozana**, Monserrate entre Obispo y Obrapía, **T** 8671033. *1200-2400. Map 2, I4, p249* The oldest restaurant in Havana, *La Zaragozana* does a great job of pulling off the Spanish theme, with wooden panelling, interior brick bar, and a smattering of Zaragoza football flags and knick-knacks. The atmosphere can be rather chilly when the a/c is pumping and the resident band isn't.

! During Columbus' second journey to the New World, he landed at Gibara in Cuba. Forays inland brought reports that the local inhabitants were smoking roughly rolled dried leaves for ceremonial or religious purposes, which they called *cohibas*. The Spaniards soon acquired the taste for tobacco and in the 17th century introduced it to the European market with great success.

Rum

Light, dry rum in Cuba is aged for three years, has little body and is between 40° and 60° proof. Old, dry rum is aged for five years, is amber in colour and can be drunk straight or added to cocktails. Extra aged rum (*ron añejo*) is aged for seven years and while occasionally added to cocktails, is usually drunk neat in a brandy glass.

Cocktails first became popular after the development of ice making in the USA in 1870 and were then introduced to Cuba. The cocktail boom came in the 1920s with an influx of bartenders and visitors from all over the world, many of whom were escaping prohibition in the USA. Many recipes were named after visiting film stars and other dignitaries and developed at *La Bodeguita del Medio* or *El Floridita*. The *Hemingway Special* was created for the writer by the famous *El Floridita* bartender, Constante. Every barman makes a slightly different mojito; some are sweeter than others, but all are refreshing, tasty and light enough to be drunk at any time. To make one, put half a tablespoon of sugar, the juice of half a lime and some lightly crushed mint leaves in a tall glass. Stir well, then add soda water, ice cubes, 1½ oz light, dry rum and top up with soda water. Serve with a garnish of mint leaves and, of course, a straw. The recipe for the daiquiri was created by an engineer in the Daiquirí mines near Santiago de Cuba in 1898. It includes the juice of half a lime, 1½ table-spoons of sugar, 1½ oz light, dry rum, some drops of maraschino liqueur and some ice, which you put in a shaker, shake and serve strained in a cocktail glass, with more ice if needed. The idea of using shaved ice came later, added by Constante in the 1920s. It was a favourite of Hemingway; he described it in *Islands in the Stream*, and drank it in the company of Jean-Paul Sartre, Gary Cooper, Tennessee Williams, Marlene Dietrich and Ava Gardner among others.

The international menu, including enchiladas and garlic prawns, is nothing to write home about, and the potentially tasty house speciality, paella, is blemished by the anaemic-looking carrots and peas, and a lack of Mediterranean touches. Good wine selection and unobtrusive friendly service.

$$ **Mesón de la Flota**, Mercaderes 257, **T** 8629281. *Map 6, F3, p256* A very sociable restaurant-cum-tapas bar with cosily clustered wooden tables, and impassioned flamenco *tablaos* after 2100 each evening. The reasonably priced menu has a wide selection of dishes, with a fish and seafood emphasis. The papaya, tuna and onion salad is a refreshing appetiser at US$3.50, but promising pesto chicken and prawn kebabs are undermined by unadvertised hunks of greasy pork. The tapas choices are good value, including deliciously feisty *patatas bravas*. The service is friendly, if a little lackadaisical.

$$-$ **Torre de Marfil**, Mercaderes entre Obispo y Obrapía, **T** 8671038. *1200-2200. Map 6, D4, p256* A favourite haunt of travellers in search of the Havana Holy Grail of Oriental cuisine. Decked out with colourful lanterns and Chinese paraphernalia, and a hit-and-miss, but generally good value menu, the *Torre de Marfil* clings to its alleged Chinese ancestry fairly credibly. House speciality dishes include Tip pan chicken, smoked pork and a pretty good stab at a chop suey. The food surpasses anything that Chinatown has to offer in terms of authenticity and salubriousness.

$ **Al Medina**, Oficios entre Obrapía y Obispo, **T** 8671041. *1200-2300. Map 6, D4, p256* The peaceful aura, lush courtyard setting, strumming guitars and chirping birds make for a relaxing evening or an escape-from-the-crowds lunchtime venue. The freshly prepared Arab food is a tasty change if you have exhausted the Cuban repertoire. Main course dishes, priced between US$4-12, include Tangier chicken served with olives and slabs of mango, sesame chicken and a huge vegetarian combo. There is a range of inspired appetisers, at US$2-3, including the old classics of houmous and falafel. Lovely fresh fruit juices, US$1, and delicious coffee. At the weekends there are regular shows at 2130.

$ Cafetería Torrelavega, Obrapía 114, next to the Casa de México. *0900-2100. Map 6, D4, p256* With shaded seating on the Parque Simón Bolívar, this no-frills, seriously cheap and cheerful café, is a handy pit-stop on the old town walkabout. Re-fuel on the US$3 special of chicken, chips, salad and coffee, or spaghetti, at US$0.65, and sandwiches from US$0.70-1. A *Cristal* beer, US$1.

$ Gentiluomo, Bernaza esquina Obispo, T 8671300.*1200-2300. Map 2, I5, p249* Unmissable, thanks to the brigade of menu-touting waiters lurking at the top of the Obispo strip, *Gentiluomo* serves passable and cheap carbohydrate fodder, with pasta and pizza ranging from US$3.50-8. A deceptively varied menu, with the lack of seasonal ingredients striking off many choices and what remains generally failing to be spruced up to full potential.

$ Hanoi, C Brasil 507 y Bernaza, T 8671029. *0700-2400. Map 2, J4, p249* Don't be duped, there is nothing remotely oriental about the setting, or the food, down at *Hanoi*. Charming, friendly and immensely popular, it is usually chock full with upbeat punters enjoying unadorned, resolutely Cuban fare in a lovely colonial set-ting, with merry, live music. The food, often bland and reheated, is served up with fast-food rapidity and style, but at bargain prices you can't really complain – three courses for US$6, *combinados* for US$2-2.50, sandwiches US$1. 50. Blast-off mojitos at US$1 are the cheapest in the old town. A mellow central spot for breakfast.

$ Puerto de Sagua, Egido 603, T 8671026. *Map 2, J4, p249* This nautical-themed restaurant just around the corner from Capitolio has two dining options and a sleek, chrome New York 1950s-style bar, which serves great cocktails. The cheaper canteen-style option lacks atmosphere but serves good value, well-prepared food with attentive service. A recommended lunchtime bite is the prawns in tomato (ask for it *piquante*) sauce at US$4, pasta napolitano, US$1.50 and pizzas, US$1.20. Next door, same kitchen, the more upscale restaurant is overpriced, but the added bonus of live musical accompaniment. Handy if you are sightseeing around Capitolio, but don't go out of your way.

Centro

Paladares

$$ **La Guarida**, Concordia 418 entre Gervasio y Escobar, **T** 8624940. *1200-2300. Map 2, F1, p248* Many a Havana paladar has risen to fame on the coat-tails of internationally acclaimed La Guarida, which is on most tourists' hit list. Firmly on the map since its appearance in Tomás Gutiérrez Alea's cinematic masterpiece *Fresa y Chocolate*, *La Guarida* serves a tantalizing synthesis of international and Cuban cuisine in a beautifully restored colonial mansion. Dishes for the health conscious, to the tune of grouper served with a zingy carrot and coconut sauce, are freshly prepared and stylistically presented. Although slightly above the average paladar price range, by international standards, this is an excellent value dining experience. Enjoy it while it lasts – there is speculation that it may soon be transformed into a hotel. Reservations essential.

$$ **La Tasquita**, Jovellar (27 de Septiembre) entre Espada y San Francisco, **T** 798647. *1200-2400. Map 3, F7, p250* Just as you imagine a Cuban paladar should be, *Santiagüeña* Arralicia serves up wonderful home cooking in a welcoming, living room-style setting embellished with lace, festive chintz and wood panelling. The hearty portions, guaranteed to cause midriff havoc, are well

prepared and wonderfully fresh. Even the familiar rice and beans are a taste sensation. Generosity also extends to the cocktail lists with kicking mojitos. The best in town for back to basics, unassuming paladar dining.

$ Paladar Bellomar, Virtudes 169A esquina Amistad, **T** 8610023. *1130-2330. Map 2, H4, p249* Glowing with fairy lights and glistening with chintz, and with the highest kitsch-factor in Havana, *Paladar Bellomar* sits like a Santa's grotto in the backstreets of central Havana. Only forget tricks or wizardry, *Bellomar* is a bastion of paladar traditionalism with good value, unadorned Cuban fare served up in an intimate family setting.

Vedado

Paladares

$$ Adela, Calle F 503 entre 21 y 23, **T** 323776. *Call ahead for opening hours. Map 3, E3, p250* Bohemian Adela's artist's abode would more likely make it into the pages of *Elle Deco*, with bottles set into the walls, a tasteful art collection, eclectic furnishings and lush terrace. The gastronomic bounty is in itself a work of art, but a nail biting experience for the budget conscious, as Adela likes to free the diner from making decisions. The appetisers, including cinnamon-baked bananas, cheese platters, fried malanga, seasoned pumpkin squash balls and corn and chorizo stew, just keep on coming ahead of the very limited main course selection (usually two). Certainly not cheap, prices can top US$20-25 per head.

$$ Hurón Azul, Humboldt 153 esquina P, **T** 791691. *1200-2400. Map 3, E7, p250* A paladar-cum-tardis if ever there was one. The immense popularity of *Hurón Azul* requires a creative use of space and an even more creative interpretation of the 12- seater rule.

This bohemian hangout is chock full of wall-to-wall eye candy with paintings by renowned local artists such as Fabelo and Nelsón Domínguez and a photo gallery of celebrities major and minor, including members of the *Fresa y Chocolate* cast. The chef is allegedly the "most creative" in Havana. There is more menu-mulling potential, including chicken in mustard sauce and Mediterranean-style fish stuffed with fresh tuna, lashings of olives, peppers and tomato. Be aware that if you nibble on the ornate fruit extravaganza on your table or unsolicited bread basket, your bill will soon exceed the standard paladar price range by far.

$ **Amor**, 23 759 entre B y C, **T** 8338150. *Mon-Fri 1900-2400. Map 3, E1, p250* One of the best paladars in Havana serving imaginative food in a refined baroque setting. Service is warm and attentive and the grandiose portions served on the Sunday best china are highly satisfying. The peanut-encrusted fried turkey and Basque-style chicken with tomato and olives are delicious. Main courses served with *congrí* are a bargain at US$8. On the first Sunday of each month *Amor* hosts the *Azotea de Elda Peña*, an informal rooftop gathering where local musicians perform, complementary wine is served and a great time is had by all. Donations to the local children's cancer hospital are greatly appreciated. *Amor* is a must.

$ **El Helecho**, 6 203 entre Línea y 11, **T** 8313552. *1900-2300. Map 4, B12, p253* Pretty hard to miss, with bright yellow canopies and a quaint Swiss-style sign post, *El Helecho* is possibly the only paladar in Havana still dealing in *moneda nacional*. The cuisine is filling, unadorned and unapologetically Cuban with a stab at a diabetic-inducing Chinese sauce. Dining occurs at the front of the house, rather frustratingly separated from the colonial treasures within, and unless local banter is in full swing, the atmosphere can be a bit church like. Main dishes with *congrí* and salad average out at a top value 162 pesos (around US$6).

$ Gringo Viejo, 21 454 entre E y F, **T** 326150. *Mon-Sat 1200-2400. Map 3, D2, p250* Lots of entrepreneurial zeal has transformed the thematically inspired *Gringo Viejo* into one of the most established Havana paladars with a regular clientèle of expats and locals. Wall-to-wall cinema memorabilia, a neat, well-stocked bar area and a warm, attentive atmosphere make this a great place to spend an evening. The standard fish, chicken and pork dishes are re-branded in a less lardy format and served up with a choice of well-prepared fruity and spicy sauces. Great value at an average US$8.50 for a main course with rice, beans and salad.

$ Le Chansonnier, J 257 entre 15 y Línea, **T** 8321576. *1900-2400. Map 3, C4, p250* A regal, pastel pink colonial mansion with first class service and all the silver service trimmings courtesy of the family entourage. There is a much healthier approach to the standard dishes, which benefits from chef Hector's French aspirations, although the duck, swamped with a gloopy cream and mushroom sauce, was more a case of ooh la lard! Veggies will delight over the bountiful fruit and vegetable salad. All main courses, served with fries and rice, are US$10. Hector and his mum, who enjoys the role of international raconteur, will gladly tip you off on the private party scene over an after dinner liqueur and cigar.

$ Los Amigos, M entre 19 y 21, opposite *Hotel Victoria*. *1200-2400. Map 3, D6, p250* A good blend of locals and tourists and a wacky mix of Christmas decorations, religious artefacts, fairy lights and wind chimes redeem the basic and greasy Cuban food. On the positive side, the rice and beans with added fried plantain

! The family firm of Bacardí was the largest in Cuba for nearly 100 years. After the 1959 Revolution, when the sugar industry and the distilleries were taken over by the state, the family left the island and took the Bacardí name with them. The Bacardí rum, now found worldwide, is not distilled in Cuba.

are delicious, the location is convenient for the après-dining entertainment of La Rampa and the prices are the cheapest in town –
that is until your amigo tries to short change you! Check your bill.

$ Los Mercedes, 18 204 entre 15 y 17. *1200-2300 Map 4, C10,
p253* More beach-side Montego Bay than colonial Vedado, this tiki
hut-style paladar squats humbly amidst the imposing mansions of
Vedado. The entrance, a mini-bridge crossing a turtle pool, and
Gloria Gaynor soundtrack sets the mood for a quirky, laid-back
evening. Fish is the speciality here, served up with plenty of saucy
options and the house dish *Filete los Mercedes* is a tasty choice.
Main course dishes with rice and salad, an average US$12.50.

$ Nerei, 19 esquina L, **T** 327860. *1200-2400. Map 3, D5,
p250* Unfortunately this great paladar loses out to the far cheaper
and inferior *Los Amigos* around the corner. With a refreshing
emphasis on grilling rather than frying, the portions are
substantial and the lovely, breezy veranda is a great place to
watch the Vedado world go by. Main dishes including lamb with
pepper, chicken and beer, turkey with wine and grilled squid, tot
up to an average US$11 with salad and rice. Cocktails are decent
but a bit steep at US$3.50. Just off 23, it is a laid-back, hassle free
start to a night out in central Vedado.

State restaurants

$$$ La Torre, 17 y M, at the top of Edif Focsa, **T** 325650.
1200-2400. Map 3, C6, p250 The apocalyptic state of the 1950s
FOCSA building with a less than shipshape elevator – an accident
in 2000 killed one person – could deter you from venturing up to
La Torre. But steel-coat the nerves and you are in for a treat. This is
the best classical French food in Havana, with great views over the
city, especially at night. US$40 per person but worth every cent.

$$$-$ Casa de la Amistad, Paseo entre 17 y 19, **T** 8308037. *1100-2300. Map 4, C12, p253* This welcoming cultural centre with a lush, tiled courtyard is a great place to hang out and wind down for a couple of hours, serenaded by a happy quartet. Reasonably priced bar snacks include fried chicken, sandwiches and pizza. Inside the main building, *Restaurant Primavera*, open 1200-2400, is an altogether more elegant affair, with fine colonial furniture, antiques, attentive, unobtrusive service – and an elevated price tag to match. In the evening there are regular *peñas*, see p156.

$$-$ La Roca, 21 102 esquina M, **T** 8334501. *1200-2300. Map 3, D6, p250* A rat-packer retro heaven, this restored 1950s art deco-style building features original stained glass windows dating back to its former days as a guest house. The sleek but stark dining area with high wooden ceilings lacks atmosphere when the punter count is low. There is an international menu for all budgets, including appetisers of chicken fajitas, US$2.95, French onion soup, US$2 and main course offerings to the tune of spaghetti carbonara with shrimps, US$5, shell fish paella, US$15, "English-style roast beef", sadly minus the Yorkshire pudding, and for dessert, a fairly well-executed rendition of Argentine *tres leches*.

$$ Polinesia, *Hotel Habana Libre*, L y 23, **T** 6554011. *1200-2400. Map 3, E5, p250* With a separate entrance on La Rampa, the smart and moody *Polinesia* serves up an aspiring mix of Chinese and Indonesian dishes in an atmospheric bamboo-clad setting. Prices are not cheap, main dishes are US$12-20, and resilient Cuban flavours seem to crop up in most dishes.

$ Cafetería La Rampa, *Hotel Habana Libre*, La Rampa. Calle 23. *24hrs. Map 3, E5, p250* *La Rampa* is a regular fall back for travellers, *Habana Libre* guests who got up too late for breakfast and a 24-hour post-party saviour. Far from sublime gastronomy, it is popular for its predictable selection of home-from-home international snacks and mojito-mopping comfort food. Breakfast, sandwiches, pizza, US$3.50 plus toppings US$1-2, and pasta (US$2.20-6), burgers (US$4.50-6.50) and main meals.

$ Coppelia, 23 y L, opposite *Hotel Habana Libre. In theory, kiosks open 24 hrs, but in reality, Tue-Sun 1100-2230. Map 3, E5, p250*
When it comes to the serious business of ice cream, queuing protocol is strictly adhered to. There are several separate outdoor areas to eat in, each with their own entrance and queue in the surrounding streets. Dedicated attendants control the queues and will direct you into the seating area as tables become free. There are separate areas for pesos and dollars. As a rule, dollar-paying tourists will be directed inside *La Torre*, which is a rather alien set up with blasting music and less Cuban mingling potential. If you are prepared to queue, which is not unpleasant as the design is integral with the characteristic copey trees; or if you can coincide your visit with a big baseball game, sitting in the communal out-door peso areas is the far more rewarding *Coppelia* cultural insight.

Bring your own plastic spoons for the tubs as they invariably run out. US$2 for small portion, many different flavours, depending on availability (chocolate is still the top flavour), and styles (all come with a glass of water): *ensalada* (mixture of flavours), *jimaguas* (twins) and *tres gracias*. After devouring your first choice you can stay and order a second portion without queuing. Alternatively, sample the *Coppelia* ice cream in the tourist hotels and restaurants and some dollar food stores. *Bim Bom*, 23 y Calzada de Infanta, Vedado, is another ice cream shop, while several street stalls specialize in ice cream (*helado*), 21 esquina K, near to *Coppelia* but no queues, 3 pesos per cone.

$ La Casona de 17, Calle 17 60 entre M y N, **T** 334529. *1200-0200. Map 3, C6, p250* This elegant peach mansion with a colonial terrace, once home to Fidel's grandparents, unfortunately faces out onto the phenomenally ugly 1950s FOCSA building. The substantial house dish is the *Paella Casona*, at US$7.50, or you can always fall back on a rather greasy half-a-roast chicken served with bacon, rice 'n beans, chips and salad. The adjoining Argentine *parillada* serves up mixed grills of all the likely contenders; fish, chicken, pork and prawns. Nice place for a relaxing lunch.

$ El Conejito, M esquina 17, **T** 8324671. *1200-2400.*
Map 3, C5, p250 Inexplicably designed like a 17th-century Tudor house, with waitresses looking like they are about to break into a spot of yodelling, *El Conejito* is quite the culinary conundrum. Rabbit is the speciality – salted, stewed, skewered or sausage-style – smothered in a variety of sauces, served up with fries, and christened with such weird and wacky names as "Rabbit à la female hunter". At an average US$6 it is good value. For fans of *Watership Down*, there are pork, chicken and seafood options. There is an adjoining 24-hour bar with karaoke, Thursday-Sunday 2000-0200.

$ Hotel Nacional de Cuba, O esquina 21, **T** 333564.
1200-1500. Map 3, D7, p250 Satisfying most cravings, the all-you-can-eat lunch-time buffet at the *Nacional* has a high quality selection of fish and meat dishes and a wonderful selection of fruit and vegetable salads. There is a cook-as-you-like pasta bar, with barrels of fresh parmesan shavings, and hunks of stilton for veggies. There is also an area devoted to boosting the sugar economy with a cream-drenched array of tarts, biscuits, puddings and ice creams. The setting is lovely with great views over the Malecón. Vegetarians can negotiate the price down from US$15 to US$10.

! In February 2002, José Castelar Cairo made it into the *Guinness Book of Records* for rolling the longest ever cigar; 11 metres long, taking nine days, and using enough tobacco leaves to produce 1,200 *Gran Coronas*. In a ceremony at Castillo de Morro, where Cairo runs a rum and cigar shop, he received his official certificate from the British ambassador, Paul Hare.

$ **Pekin**, Calle 12 y 23, close to Cementerio Colón, **T** 334020. *1200-2300. Map 4, D11, p253* Vegetarians have had a notoriously raw deal in Cuba, and if you have withdrawal symptoms for greens, this could be the answer. The initiative of the Minister of Commerce, allegedly an ardent vegetarian, this peso restaurant serves up more than 50 vegetable dishes on a buffet-style spread. Aubergines stuffed with soya, veggie paella, lasagne, salads, sautéed spinach, stir fried cauliflower, sticky puds, juices and soups, etc. Great for the waistline and the budget, you can fill a couple of trays for less than 40 pesos, US$1.60. The catch, of course, is that there are usually huge queues and slow service, the food is cold, tepid at best and the selection usually shrinks from 50 dishes to two by 2200. The best branch is on Calzada, entre D y E, in the loveliest area of Vedado, with pleasant outdoor seating, great views of Teatro Amadeo Roldán, and smaller queues.

$ **Trattoria Marakas**, O entre 23 y 25, **T** 333640. *1200-2400. Map 3, E6, p250* Belonging to the *Hotel St John*, this diner-cum-school canteen dishes up a broad and inspired line up of credible Italian food, including gnocchi with smoked salmon and cream and a passable pesto. The prices aren't bad with pizzas US$3.95-US$5.75 and pasta dishes US$5 average, and there's the added bonus of olive oil and balsamic vinegar on the tables. The plastic furniture and insipid pastel-green paintwork don't exactly give you the impression you are in Rome.

Miramar

Paladares

$ **La Cocina de Liliam**, Calle 48 1311 entre 13 y 15, **T** 296514. *Sun-Fri 1200-1500, 1900-2200, closed Dec. Map 4, D2, p252* If this is your first initiation into the delights of paladar dining be aware that you may peak too soon. Each dish is served imaginatively and in abundance by Lilliam, the Martha Stewart of Havana, in the beautiful, pre-Raphaelite courtyard of this Miramar mansion. The prices are great value at around US$8.50 for a main course. The red snapper brochette, served atop sticky white rice and a crunchy salad with aromatic dressing, is highly recommended. There is a great selection of tasty appetizers including malanga fritters, chickpea platters and home-made onion bread with olive oil.

$ **La Esperanza**, Calle 16 105 entre 1 y 3, **T** 224361. *1200-1600, 1900-2330, closed Wed. Map 4, A6, p252* Another top night, top nosh Miramar experience. The atmosphere is pure Almodóvar, the food and attitude is pseudo-Parisien. The varied and ever-changing menu delivered at lightning speed by the brusque Herbert may leave you plucking for the only thing that you can remember, but each dish is a delightful deviation from traditional Cuban fare. Delicious main course dishes include seared tuna steaks with roasted red peppers and breast of chicken in caramelized orange sauce. Clearly fans of all things fruity, Herbert and Manolo also whip up good, highly potent mango daiquiris.

$ **Calle 10**, Calle 10 314 entre 3 y 5, near Teatro Karl Marx, **T** 296702. *1200-2400. Map 4, E7, p253* Another very professional set up, the residents of Calle 10 certainly know how to cultivate a jovial holiday vibe, with the added bonus of being one of the cheapest of the Miramar crop. The well-prepared food leans towards Cuban, with the old shredded beef favourite, *ropa vieja*, taking star billing alongside plenty of pork. There is the odd international twist, including grilled fish with a white wine and seafood sauce, and a great salad Niçoise. Great setting with out-door eating area with open air grill, tiki bar, upbeat tunes and gas-tronomic props including strewn onions and garlic, which unfortunately don't keep away the dollar-sucking minstrels – don't ask for change from your US$10.

State restaurants

$$$ Tococoro, Calle18 302 esquina 3ra, **T** 2042209. *1200-2400. Map 4, B5, p252 Tococoro* is set in a beautiful colonial building, eclectically decorated with murals, inscribed wooden butcher's-style blocks on the walls, paintings and antique furnishings. The tropical, Tococoro bird-themed dining room is an intimate, unpretentious setting with high standards of service and innovative cooking, but at a price. There is no menu, only the "chef's choices of the day". Previous diners include Gabriel García Márquez, Matt Dillon and Jane Fonda. *Tococoro* recently opened the *Salón Japonés*, featuring the Sakura sushi bar serving refreshingly digestible Japanese food, washed down with highly quaffable saki.

$$$-$$ 1830, Av 7 1252 entre 20 y 22. *1200-2400. Map 4, B9, p253* The high-class *1830* offers sumptuous dining options, cabaret shows and a top line up of local bands, in a wonderful setting at the mouth of the Río Almendares. The menu offers a creative synthesis of French and Cuban flavours. Prices vary from US$12.50, for fish with lime and capers, to US$15.25 for tenderloin with blue cheese sauce and lobster at US$25. Don't miss the Sala Japonesa, an imitation 'Japanese island', made entirely of stones and shells with alcoves and alleyways, the romantic setting for wedding and *quinceañera* celebrations. Visiting celebrities have included Alicia Alonso, Raúl Castro and Alejo Carpentier. *1830* is a must if only to sample an industrial-strength cocktail in the *Mesón de la Chorrera* bar, which has fantastic views over the river. There is cabaret every night from 2200; call ahead for the line-up and admission prices.

$ El Ajibe, Av 7 entre 24 y 26, **T** 2044233. *1200-2300. Map 4, C5, p252* Another Havana institution, *El Ajibe* is a big favourite with locals, travellers, businessmen, artists and celebrities who come in droves to enjoy the house speciality – chicken marinated in tangy orange sauce. The breezy, open framework setting is a great lunchtime spot, and the service is friendly and attentive. With second helpings of chips, beans and rice, this is top value at an average US$12.

Playa

Paladares

$$$ La Ferminia, Av 3 esquina 18, **T** 336555. *1200-2400. Map 1, p247* A beautiful neoclassical residence with an elegant atmosphere. With an emphasis on the use of natural ingredients and cooking methods, this Havana gastronomic institution is also a training school for budding chefs, which may explain the rather hit-and-miss cuisine. La Ferminia is one of the best mid-range restaurants for vegetarians with tasty veggie pies, a clutch of pasta options and an all-you-can vegetarian buffet. For the more carnivorous there is a good value *churrasquería,* all-you-can eat skewers of prime Uruguayan meat, served with chips and rice for US$12.95 in the lovely courtyard garden.

The Revolution may have curbed the debauched excesses of the Fabulous Fifties, but Havana's brand of rum-fuelled hedonism still lures mega stars and tourists to its vibrant clubs and bars. Vedado has the lion's share of clubs and musical venues, from the swanky to the seedy, while Miramar and Playa is the locale for titillating cabaret and raunchy discos. La Habana Vieja is brimming with bars, tango houses and cultural centres. The main strip of Calle Obispo is the place to begin an old town bar hop, where a seductive musical soundtrack and spontaneous streetside grooving provides some of the city's best free entertainment. As the bars close at 2400, the clubs get into full swing, continuing until the early hours. You should expect queues at the weekends. For Cubans a night on the tiles means serious sartorial grooming and most clubs have a smart dress code, strictly enforced by the door staff. In theory, no one under 18 is admitted, although many places are frequented by *jineteros* bringing a less than wholesome feel to the proceedings.

The emphasis is on dancing, be it salsa and Latin dance styles, R&B, hip hop or rock. Most venues now feature matinées, aimed at young Cubans with entrance in pesos, which have a more authentic vibe. It's always worth checking out the cream of Havana's hotels, which provide the venue for big name bands. The *Nacional* usually has a great Saturday night line-up with home-grown Grammy winning favourites *Los Van Van* often taking time out from the global circuit. Prices start at US$25, or including dinner US$40. See p140.

Bars

La Habana Vieja

Bar Dos Hermanos, Av del Puerto esquina Santa Clara, **T** 8613514. *24 hours. Map 6, H4, p256* Close to the ferry terminal, the *Two Brothers Bar* works hard to maintain its more sporadic tourist trade. Claiming, like many, to be the oldest bar in Havana, this is a great down-to-earth saloon-style bar, popular with locals and straying tourists. The cocktails are excellent value and the reasonable food is served with more care and attention than most of the tourist magnets around Obispo. Long-term travellers swear by the *Pollo dos Hermanos* at US$2.85 washed down by a top value US$1.50 mojito. This is a great spot to watch the sun come up and tuck into a post-party breakfast.

Bar Monserrate, Monserrate esquina Obrapía. *1100-2400. Map 2, I4, p249* Just off Parque Central, the decor and ambience is as familiar as the clientele, with woody furnishings, high ornate ceilings, draping plants, hypnotic fans and music to watch the world go by. With good views of the *Gran Teatro*, this is an upbeat joint to soak up the pretty average cocktails, at an above average US$3, or a local *Cristal* at US$1, and survey the Parque Central hullabaloo.

The stodgy set menus, including fried chicken, bean soup, rice, salad, dessert and coffee are good value at US$6.50, but not the kind of munchies to keep you light on your feet all night – best avoided. Pop next door to *El Castillo de Farnés* restaurant instead.

Bar Nostalgia, Oficios 53 esquina Obrapía. *2100-0200.*
Map 6, E4, p256 Intimate, cellar-like space tucked away on the first floor of *Hostal Valencia*. Great late-night spot to relax, kick back and enjoy live salsa, trova, timba and son from the resident musicians. The Saturday line-up usually like to market their *Buena Vista* connections – *"Los 50 en Strike"*, the grandchildren of Compay Segundo, and revered clan member himself Barbarito Torres. If your Spanish is up to it, there are slap dash, Benny Hill-style 'comic' interludes, or a better option is to nip downstairs for the best paella in Havana at *Restaurante La Paella*, see p129.

Bilbao, O'Reilly entre Cuba y Aguiar *Map 6, C2, p256* A shrine to Atlético Bilbao, this earthy peso bar just off the main drag can be an interesting take on La Habana Vieja. Not enough greenback potential here to lure the local musical talent, so you may have to settle for renditions of *Unchained Melody* and other tunes from less righteous brothers. Depending on the moment, and your fellow barflies, this can be a more authentic and thought-provoking old town experience. You will pay in pesos but at a tourist dollar equivalent, so go for experience not for economy.

Bosque de Bologna, Obispo entre Villegas y Aguacate.
1100-0100. Map 2, I5, p249 The 'Wood of Bologna' with its tranquil courtyard setting and absentee *jineteros* makes a peaceful time-out from the Obispo action. Service is friendly and the imitation Italian food, including the house special *Pollo Bologna*, chicken with stir-fried seafood, is generally superior and lighter on the gut than most other culinary offerings on the strip. There is live music Monday-Friday 0600-2200 and on Saturday and Sunday 1200-2200.

Casa del Escabeche, Obispo esquina a Villegas, **T** 8632660.
0800-2400. Map 2, I5, p249 This tiny, welcoming bar is easy to
spot by the overflow of upbeat, smiley punters spilling out onto
Obispo day and night. The excellent house quartet kicks off at
noon each day, and you won't be able to hover in the wings long
before you are invited to join in the spatially challenged grooving
and girating. Definitely number one on any La Habana Vieja bar
crawl. Cracking cocktails for US$1.50.

Café de París, Obispo 202 esquina San Ignacio. *0800-2400.
Map 6, C3, p256* The predominantly tourist clientele who flock to
Café de Paris makes it a prime stomping ground for every Obispo
jinetero. Be prepared, tourist-weary, assumptive bartenders will
often pre-empt your second round of mojitos at a none-too-cheap
US$3.00 a throw. A place where most things come unsolicited, but
the location, quality of the music and the people-watching potential make it worthwhile.

El Castillo de Farnés, Av de Monserrate esquina Obrapía,
T 8671030. *24 hours. Map 2, I4, p249* A lively hangout, a stone's
throw from the action of Obispo and Parque Central. Plenty of
action late afternoon when the street life outside competes for
airwave domination with the musical talent and chattering
punters inside. The bar serves cheap snacks and an OK breakfast,
but avoid the additional (tap) water you will be served with your
coffee. Often overlooked is the convivial Spanish restaurant tucked
away behind the bar where Castro came at 0445, 9 January 1959.
Particularly recommended are the tasty *garbanzos* and shrimps.

El Floridita, on the corner of Obispo and Monserrate, next to the
Parque Central, **T** 631060. *1130-2400. Map 2, I5, p249*
The proclaimed "cradle of the daiquiri", any attempts to break with
tourist protocol and order anything but Big Ern's favourite tipple is
likely to be met with total horror. Despite the extensive cocktail list,

Bars and clubs

★ **Best drinks with a view**

- *Turquino, Hotel Habana Libre*, p162.
- *El Delirio Habanero*, p157.
- *La Terraza, Hotel Nacional*, p140.
- *Poolside bar, Hotel Parque Central*, p105.
- *Roof Garden Bar, Hotel Ambos Mundos*, p151.

and their legendary status, the barmen's credentials clearly go unchallenged. The plush, red velvet decor, squidgy sofas and Hemingway memorabilia would make it a perfect spot for loung-ing around if it wasn't for the wallet-raiding US$6 cocktails.

El Louvre, Prado 416 entre San Raphael y San Miguel, **T** 8608595. *Map 2, H4, p249* The street level *El Louvre* bar at the *Hotel Inglaterra* is a great early evening vantage point for Parque Central people watching. Historically, a meeting place for bohemians and revolutionaries, nowadays celebrities, artists and tourists are lured by the resident musicians, usually at full throttle from 1700. The daiquiris are generous and well priced at US$2, and highly quaffable after the half-an-hour wait; service is notoriously slow.

Fundación Distilería Havana Club, Av del Puerto 262 entre Sol y Muralla, **T** 8618051. *1000-2400. Map 6, H4, p256* The rum museum's classy, 1930s cellar-style *Bar Havana Club* is definitely the place to abandon the *Silver Dry* cocktails and develop your purist's palette with a personal appreciation of the *Havana Club* ageing process. The chosen tipple has to be the 15-year-old reserve, smoothed down with a *Cohiba* for a classic 1930s moment. If your cash is burning a hole in your pocket, splash out on the exclusive special edition *Habana Club Solera San Cristóbal*, only sold here in the club distillery. Playing on the old time bohemian theme, there are regular son performances, minstrel's shows and happy hours with two cocktails for the price of one. The restaurant *El Café Cubano* serves reasonably priced international and Cuban dishes with great chicken skewers.

Hotel Ambos Mundos, Obispo153 esquina Mercaderes. *1000-2300. Map 6, D3, p256* For great views of Havana, a relaxed setting and one of the most punchy daiquiris in the city, the *Roof Garden Bar* at the Two Worlds Hotel is a classic Havana moment. Additional entertainment value includes a trip in the original rickety 1950s elevator, which climbs past Hemingway's 5th floor residence, where he lived 1929-39, penning the opening chapters of *For Whom The Bell Tolls*, before he moved out to Finca Vigía. Best times to visit are at sunset and 2100, when the ceremonial cannons are fired across the bay from Castillo del Morro.

La Bodeguita del Medio, Empedrado entre San Ignacio y Mercaderes, **T** 8338857. *Map 6, B3, p256* More than a bar, *La Bodeguita* has become a museum piece to the Hemingway era and 1940s bohemia. Tour groups arrive en masse to read the scrawled vignettes that cover the walls, including Papa's famous line "*mi mojito en La Bodeguita, mi daiquiri El Floridita*". At a shell-out rate of US$6 for a less than mind-blowing mojito, it's not surprising that the true spirit of bohemian decadence has been diluted. The person who left his own literary legacy "Pete you fat bastard" on the wall, alongside the signatures of Fidel and Nat King Cole, was clearly unmoved.

La Dichosa, Obispo esquina Compostela. *0800-2400. Map 2, I6, p249* Another snug Obispo stop-off point that owes its success to the hypnotic pulling power of the resident musicians rather than

! A Cubanito is a Cuban version of a Bloody Mary, with ice, lime juice, salt, Worcester sauce, chilli sauce, light, dry rum and tomato juice. The latter is not always available.

the pseudo-chic green canopies and incongruous flower and doilies table adornments. But the comparative lack of hustling, generally unobtrusive, friendly vibe and good cocktails, enhance its lingerability and credentials for an uninterrupted conversation.

La Lluvia de Oro, Obispo esquina Habana. *0800-2400. Map 6, C1, p256* With its long, shiny wooden bar, circulating fans, perky cocktails and gyrating musicians this is the place to pitch up and take in La Habana Vieja. Mid-afternoon is when the salsa is at full pelt, shattering the often vault-like ambience. The crowd is mostly guidebook-flicking tourists, with the inevitable crop of *jineteros* touting their services to the palest of prey.

Mirador de la Bahía, Obispo 61, Plaza de Armas. *Map 6, D5, p256.* By day, this sun trap, on the roof terrace of the Natural History Museum, is a leisurely spot to soak up the sun and take in the panoramic, unobscured views of La Habana Vieja. For a great pre-dinner appetizer, head up in the evening for one of the best vantage points for the ceremonial blast off from the cannons of Castillo del Morro at 2100. The bar/restaurant serves great potent mojitos and also rather overpriced snacks and meals.

O'Reilly, O'Reilly 203 entre Cuba y San Ignacio. *24 hours. Map 6, C3, p256* A welcoming bar, with lots of greenery and tweeting birds, set on two floors overlooking bustling O'Reilly. Make a dash for the balconies overlooking the street before the *Havanatur* groups arrive for their mojito moment. The band, which looks like a bunch of Maradona clones, usually tunes up on cue for the tourist carousel. Food is cheap and cheerful with pizzas and pasta from US$1.50 or if you want to push the boat out you can try the "Thigh

! An Ernest Hemingway Special is light dry rum, grapefruit juice, maraschino liqueur, lime and shaved ice, blended and served like a daiquiri.

of the sea" fish combo with a side order of "batter-fried pork shunks" – an artery-hardening delight.

Clubs

La Habana Vieja

Casa de las Infusiones, Oficios entre Obispo y Obrapía, *1100-2400. Free. Map 6, D4, p256* Just off Plaza de Armas, the tea house provides around-the-clock musical beats from old time maestros, and up-and-coming talent, to a happy crowd of tourists and local devotees. With plenty of seating, this is a great, unpretentious and relatively hassle-free place to mingle and relax.

Casarón del Tango, Jústiz 21 entre Baratillo y Oficios, **T** 8610822. *Varied opening hours. Map 6, E4, p256* Just off the Plaza de Armas, the *Tango House* is a welcoming place to enjoy shows, take dance classes, meet people and relax. Saturday 2130-2400 headlines passionate performances from Tango all stars Emilio Alvarez, Katy Angel and Jorge Luis del Cabo. Wednesday and Friday1700-1900 feature amateur performances aimed at cultural promotion. Drop in tango classes and courses are run on Thursdays 1600-1700.

Centro de Cultura de Habana Vieja, Aguiar entre Amargura y Teniente Rey, **T**8634860. *Free. Map 6, D1, p256* This vibrant and welcoming cultural centre in southern La Habana Vieja has a varied programme but its musical *peñas* are the major draw for locals. Rumba courtesy of Tambor llévame contigo takes place on the second and fourth Saturday of the month 1800-2200. Tuesday 2000-2200 is bolero night, while on the first and third Sunday of the month 1800-2030 the *roquero* youth crank it up with rap gigs.

Don Giovanni, outside *Don Giovanni* restaurant. *Nightly from 2300, except Wed. Free.* Map 6, C4, p256 Open-air, live salsa venue popular with Cubans priced out of the dollar clubs and bars and often trying their hand at hustling the drop-by tourists. Free entertainment line-up of jovial music, vigorous dancing and a bloke who has a peculiar talent for being able to spin huge wheely bins. There is a heavy, but not threatening police presence.

Palacio de la Artesanía, Cuba 64 entre Peña Pobre y Cuarteles. *US$3 consumo mínimo.* Map 2, H7, p247 This beautiful courtyard setting makes for a mellow, *jinetero*-free Sunday spot, to hear live music from 2130-0200. Son Catedral are a frequent attraction running the gamut of Cuban musical genres. There is a friendly intimate vibe with plenty of audience engagement.

Palermo, San Miguel y Amistad. *Mon-Sun 2100-0300, Sat 2100-0400. US$2.* Map 2, H3, p249 Amid the Centro rubble, just off the main tourist drags, Palermo delivers the requisite cabaret show, nightly from 2400. Popular with young Cubans, groupies flock to the weekend showcase feature of Odelquis Revé y su changüí, Cuba's answer to Barry White, then groove to the youth club-style salsa disco.

Centro

Casa de la Cultura del Centro Habana, Av Salvador Allende 720 entre Soledad y Castillejo, **T** 8784727. Borysmundo@yahoo.com for details or call ahead. *Hours vary according to schedule of events.* Map 3, I7, p251 Budding talent literally springing up from the ruins of this dilapidated mansion. There is an extensive programme from blasting rock on the first Sunday of the month,

! A Havana Special is pineapple juice, light, dry rum, mara
schino liqueur and ice, shaken and strained.

from 1500, to sedate *peñas campesinos* on Saturday evenings from 2100, and the fourth Sunday of the month climax, from 1500, where frenetic rap and hip hop threatens literally to bring the house down.

Casa de La Trova, San Lázaro entre Belascoaín y Gervasio.*1800-2400. Free. Map 2, E2, p248* In the heart of the musical Cayo Hueso district, for going local this is a great unpretentious hang-out to hear traditional high-calibre Cuban music among a highly appreciative crowd. Line-up varied, but authentic Cuban feel guaranteed. Slot in the Friday afternoon session from 1800.

Callejón de Hamel, Hamel entre Aramburu y Hospital. *Map 3, H7, p251* La Rumba de Cayo Hueso, every Sunday from 1200-1500, is an unmissable feast of fast, kicking rumba show and electric jam sessions, which draws huge crowds of tourists and the local community. Invited guests, an artistic community feel and a responsive audience make this a hot venue. There is a small bar in the street, selling a strong drink of rum and honey, US$2. Pack lots of sunscreen and water, as they often run out.

Casarón del Tango, Neptuno 309 entre Aguila y Italia, **T** 8630097. *Mon from 1700. Map 2, H3, p249* Achingly sentimental, this musical venue-cum-museum houses a fascinating collection of tango memorabilia dating back to the 1940s, from record sleeves to all manner of Carlos Gardel idolatry. Monday afternoons from 1700 is the time to hear octogenarians, including local legend Rafael del Campo, perform heart-wrenching tango.

La Madriguera, Quinta de los Molinos entre Infanta y Salvador, **T** 8798175. *0800-1700. Peso admission is variable, if anything. Map 3, H5, p251* This wild, unruly park is furtive ground for the flourishing talents of the committed youth members of UNEAC, see p158. Cited as being *"un lugar oculto para las ideas abiertas"*,

Bars and clubs

(a hidden place for open ideas), it offers arts, crafts and musical workshops for all ages and talents. Crossing the Cuban musical spectrum, there are impassioned musicals, including hip hop, rap, rumba and more traditional Cuban rhythms. Fascinating glimpse into Cuban youth culture.

Vedado

Café Cantante, Teatro Nacional, Paseo de la Revolución, Paseo y 39, **T** 796011. *US$10 min, matinees 10 pesos. Map 3, J1, p251* Start your night in *El Delirio*, see p157, then head down to the basement for the last hour of *Café Cantante*. The doorman may let you in free of charge at this late hour. Funky crowd of fashionistas and poseurs slink, sashay and jump around to diverse Cuban beats, cranked up well into the early hours. This is a highly regarded venue, popular with local musicians and other cultural notables. Top live bands often play here and there are matinée salsa discos.

Café El Gato Tuerto, O entre 17 y 19, **T** 552696/662224. *2400-0500. US$5 consumo mínimo. Map 3, C6, p250* A 50s bohemian haunt, the sleek, post-modern, *One-Eyed Cat* is a fashionable medley of swaggering Cuban nouveaux riches and hip funksters, bordering on pretentious. The musical line-up swings heavily towards *filín* and boleros performed by local legends including Alina Torres. Elena Burke frequently received star billing here before her death in June 2002. An intimate stage set up with audience participation encouraged, so choose your seat with care!

Casa de la Amistad, Paseo 406 entre 17 y 19, **T** 303114. *US$3 admission plus US$2 consumo mínimo. Map 4, C12, p253* One of the best settings in Havana for listening to great traditional music with a welcoming atmosphere. A traditional son group, La Peña del Chan Chan, plays every Tuesday at 2100. Compay Segundo sometimes appears with the band, although he is often on tour.

Following the show there is dancing on the veranda or in the gardens, Tuesday until 2400 and Saturday to 0200. Thursday is trova night from 1800 and Saturday is *Noche Cubana* with son and guaracha. A good Cuban and tourist mix and soliciting is rare.

El Delirio Habanero, Teatro Nacional, Plaza de la Revolución, Paseo y 39, **T** 335713. *US$10* consumo mínimo. *Map 3, J1, p251* A not-to-be-missed Havana experience, the supremely tasteful *El Delirio* has a fantastic setting with great views over the Plaza. The atmosphere is intimate, the crowd unpretentious and the music uplifting. Thursday and Saturday are when the talented Los Tres Habaneros take centre stage, playing to a mixed-aged crowd of impassioned salsa devotees. The US$10 *consumo mínimo* admission is a great deal with delicious cocktails and attentive waiter service. Good value snacks are served, and if you haven't reserved a table it's worth arriving early to stake your claim for the best seats in the house, the squashy red sofas by the windows. If you haven't had your salsa fill by 0200 head downstairs for a final sweaty hour at *Café Cantante*, see p156.

El Gran Palenque Bar, 4 entre Calzada y 5. *US$5. Map 4, A12, p253* On Saturday afternoons at 1500, the peaceful courtyard of this open-air, laid-back café/bar is taken over by the acclaimed Conjunto Folklórico Nacional de Cuba for an upbeat rumba show. For percussion, salsa, and singing classes with Conjunto professionals see p177.

El Pico Blanco, *Hotel St John*, Calle O 206 entre 23 y 25, **T** 333740. *Tue-Sun 2200-0300. Map 3, E7, p250* Spectacular rooftop setting, predictable variety show of Cuban slap dash comedy followed by an unrestrained salsa disco. US$6 buys you the rights to an open bar for the evening. It's worth shelling out the weekend US$5 admission for a finer appreciation of sultry *filín* and bolero, if you are that way inclined.

Havana Café, *Hotel Mélia Cohiba*, Paseo entre 1 y 3, **T** 333636. *2100-0200. US$10 min. Map 4, A12, p253* Havana's answer to Planet Hollywood, Planet Havana loses its soul in favour of polished American 1950s pastiche. The suave New York lounge-style seating area is furnished with a centrepiece replica *Air Cubana* jet. The tassle-shaking cabaret show kicks off from 2100. The vibe is inevitably touristy, owing to the pricey cover and the crop of *Mélia* guests not venturing off base. The bar serves overpriced, US$6, poorly executed, cocktails. If money is no issue, Sunday is the best night, US$25 cover, when top local bands, including NG La Banda, draw a more impassioned audience.

Hurón Azul, Calle 17 351 entre Presidentes y H, **T** 324152. *Free. Map 3, D3, p250* The headquarters of UNEAC (artists and writers union) is housed in a majestic, colonial mansion. An inviting intelligentsia hang-out, the lovely, welcoming bar hosts regular upbeat afternoon peñas. Wednesdays alternate between nueva trova and kicking rumba, 1700-2000. Sundays feature son or rumba from 1700, and Saturdays get more sultry with bolero 2100-0100. Popular with aspiring local bohos and visiting artistic talent, this is a very civilized spot for the meeting of minds and musical energy.

Imágenes, Calzada 602 esquina C, **T** 333606. *2130-0300. US$5 consumo mínimo. Map 3, B1, p250* A chi-chi French restaurant during its pre-revolutionary belle époque, this intimate, classy piano bar is a great place for a low-key evening. Kicking things off on the smooth side, 2130-2300, is local pianist maestro Mario Romeu, followed by nuevo imagen – the showcase for budding musical talent – and call-the-talent-police karaoke until 0130. The raunchy salsa disco until 0300 makes for a fun evening climax. Bargain US$1.50 cocktails.

Bars and clubs

Jazz Café, Galerías del Paseo esquina 1, **T** 553475. *1000-0200. US$10* consumo mínimo. *Map 4, A12, p253* A sleek and savvy venue with class acts, a laid-back welcoming ambience and a highly appreciative audience. The star-studded line up includes legendary pianist Chucho Valdés, and the US$10 *consumo mínimo* is easy to satisfy, with inspired bartenders serving up punchy, price-conscious cocktails for US$2. A top night for jazz lovers.

Las Bulerías, Calle L entre 23 y 25, **T** 8323283. *1200-0400. Map 3, E5, p250* This pseudo-tapas bar, just off La Rampa, looks rather like a Lloret de Mar souvenir shop has exploded all over the walls. The serve-yourself tapas bar is a psychedelic spread of glow-in-the-dark chorizo, spongy tortilla and a gnarled leg of, allegedly, parma ham. During the week, from 2300, aspiring John Lennons and Ricky Martins take to the stage, unabashed, for karaoke – and at the weekend from 2300, *Las Bulerías* turns the lightening down low, gets the glitter balls spinning and the live salsa pumping, until 0400.

La Zorra y el Cuervo, 23 y O, **T** 662402. *2100-0400. US$5. Map 3, E6, p250* The *Fox and the Crow* is one of the best nights in Havana for jazz enthusiasts. The small cellar space on La Rampa is entered through a fine red reproduction British telephone box. A very popular club with high-calibre jazz musicians playing to an appreciative mixed crowd. Advisable to get there before 2300 if you want a table with an unobscured view of the stage. Cuban bands often feature visiting US musicians.

Tikoa, 23 entre N y O. *2100-0300. US$3. Map 3, E6, p250* Popular with travellers and locals, this small and sweaty basement club swings between a strong Afro-Cuban vibe, with Monday night rumba shows, and upbeat salsa all week long. There are also week-end matinées, 1600-2000 at $0.50, with a more spiced local flavour.

Miramar and the suburbs

Casa de la Música Egrem, Calle 20 3388 esquina 35,
T 2040447. *Matinées, Tue-Sun 1600-2000, Sun 1600-2000. US$5 (40
pesos for locals). CD shop 2200-2430. Map 4, E5, p252* One of the
top venues to listen to the cream of Havana musical talent. High
admission costs for the evening sessions unfortunately rule out the
locals and an authentic vibe. Wednesday nights are very popular and
often headlines a long and steamy set of danceable salsa tunes
delivered by the ebullient and medallion-clad Adalberto Alvarez y Su
Son. NG La Banda with their streetwise earthy lyrics, often play on
Friday, drawing an older, tour group crowd. Music kicks off at 2330.
Friday admission is US$10-US$15 depending on who plays. Mojitos
US$4. Bargain afternoon matinées are a generally more Cuban affair
with locals packed like sardines onto the small dance floor.

Macumba, Calle 222 esquina 37, La Coronela, in La Giraldilla tourist complex in the western suburbs, **T** 330568. *2100-0500. US$10
Sun-Thu, US$15 Fri-Sat, or inclusive dinner and show with bottle of
rum and 4 cokes is US$35. Map 1, p247* Rated as a top Havana
nightspot, this open-air disco has two large dance floors for salsa,
merengue and R&B and features a small floor show. It is very
popular with Cubans and foreigners, so expect queues. Tuesday
features Latin jazz and salsa with performances from local
favourites Dan Den and NG La Banda. Thursday is carnival night.

Salón Boleros en Dos Gardenias, Av 7 esquina 26, **T** 2042353.
2230-0300. US$10. Map 4, C4, p252 If golden age, soulful bolero is
to your liking then this is a top night. The all-star line up includes
renowned bolero heavyweights Alfredo Martínez and Lino Borges.

! The *Salón Rosado de Beny Moré* appeared in the 1997
Guinness Book of Records. More than 100 bands participated
in the longest ever son performance, which lasted five days.

With a mellow, intimate, old time setting it is popular with tourists and Miramar movers and shakers. There are two live performances each night. Definitely the place to dress the part. For pre-show dining, there are decent and reasonably priced restaurants.

Salón Rosado de Beny Moré, **El Tropical**, Av 41 y 46, **T** 290985. *Tue-Sun. US$5 min depending on the line up. Map 4, G5, p252* Seriously raunchy, this massively popular dance venue features some of the best salsa in town, courtesy of a top quality line-up, including the likes of Los Van Van. Unfortunately a local (peso)/tourist (dollar) segregation policy is applied. Pandemonium ensues when big name bands take a break from international touring and play here to impassioned *habaneros*, usually priced out of such spectacles by top dollar prices. It's advisable to cab it door to door, and not hang around too long at pile-out time. This is a sketchy location, and recent scuffles have led to an increased police presence. There are cabaret shows during the week and afternoon matinées on Sundays.

Cabaret

Vedado

Parisien, *Hotel Nacional*, **T** 333564/7. *Fri-Wed 2100-0230. US$30. Reservations advised. Map 3, D7, p250* An excellent show that lasts longer than *Tropicana* and is of an equivalent standard.

Salón Rojo, *Hotel Caprí*, 21 y N, **T** 333747. *US$10. Map 3, D6, p250* This is a *Tropicana*-style show with a disco afterwards until 0400; all drinks are included in the admission. Synonymous with 1950s Mafia wheeling and dealing, the *Caprí* was Meyer Lansky and Lucky Luciano's turf and in the realms of fiction it was the stomping ground of the mother of all mobsters, Don Corleone.

Scenes from the *Godfather II* were shot in the *Caprí*, which is closed until the end of 2003 for renovation work.

Turquino, 25th floor of the *Hotel Habana Libre*, **T** 8334011. *2230-0400, cabarets start at 2300 and 0100. US$15-20. Map 3, E5, p250* Great setting with amazing views from the 25th floor. The roof opens and you can dance under the stars. The very sleek NY-style bar serves expensive drinks at US$6. Live bands often play to a rather apathetic group of nouveaux riches Cubans and tourists. Unaccompanied males are likely to be fleeced as soon as they walk through the door.

Marianao

Tropicana, Calle 72 No 4504 entre 43 y 45, Marianao, reservations **T** 270110/279147 between 1000-1600. *2100-0200, closed Mon. US$70 for show and a 3-course meal, or US$60 for the show and a quarter bottle of rum and coke. Map 4, H1, p252* Since it opened in 1939, the world-renowned *Tropicana* has become a shrine to tropical sexuality. Surviving the post-revolutionary culling of US neocolonialist symbols of sin, it is now a big tourist attraction. Two hundred dancing queens shake their tassles, ruffle their feathers and let it all well and truly hang out in this fleshy feast. The heavily choreographed routine is performed to tunes that run the gamut of Cuban musical genres. With an open-air setting, known as *Paradise Under the Stars*, you get your money back if it rains. There is a disco until the wee small hours. It is best to take a tour, which includes transport, as a taxi from La Habana Vieja costs US$12.

Havana must be one of the most culturally rich and exciting cities in the world, leading the field in the quality and quantity of its home grown music, dance, ballet, cinema and other artistic spheres. The Revolution encouraged the arts to develop a national identity but under the cloak of censorship. There is a national dance company, symphony orchestra and opera. International companies and artistes visit regularly, often as part of a festival of drama, music or dance. Events take place during the day as well as far into the night so you'll never be short of something to do or see. There are also performances for children, such as puppets at the Teatro Guiñol. Cuban cinema is unbeatable and you will probably be able to catch up with some golden oldies as well as the latest releases. The newspaper, *Opciones*, has a listing of what's on as does *Cartelera*, available free of charge, every Thursday, and found at most hotel receptions. Radio Taíno FM 93.3, English and Spanish language tourist station, gives details of venues and Cuban bands playing, particularly in the programme *El Exitazo Musical del Caribe* from 1500-1800.

Cinema

One of the great success stories of the Revolution is the Cuban film industry. Films shot on location, with hand-held cameras featuring ordinary people engaged in a revolutionary process, are the trademarks of classic Cuban cinema. In the 1960s films were national, nonconformist and cheap. In the 1970s, films tended to focus on women's issues, historical and/or multiracial themes, while in the 1980s the increasing influence of the Hollywood format brought sentimental melodrama and romance, but was critical of Cuban social reality.

The most successful film ever made was *Fresa y Chocolate* (Strawberry and Chocolate) in 1993 by leading director **Tomás Gutiérrez Alea**. The film that has made the greatest impact in recent years is without doubt Wim Wender's *Buena Vista Social Club* (1998), a nostalgic musical documentary of the band whose original members are now in their eighties and nineties.

Two recent films to look out for are *Miel para Oshún* (2001, Honey for the Goddess Oshun), by veteran filmmaker **Humberto Solás** – a story of a Cuban, Roberto, who was taken to the USA as a child after the Revolution and returns 30 years later to find his mother, and **Juan Carlos Tabío**'s comedy, *Lista de Espera* (2001, Waiting List). The action takes place in a remote, dilapidated bus station. All the buses pass full, so the passengers try to repair an old Soviet wreck in a collective effort to repair the broken dream.

The most controversial film recently about Cuba is **Julian Schabel**'s *Before Night Falls* (2001), loosely based on the autobiography of gay Cuban writer Reinaldo Arenas' *Antes que anochezca*, see p222.

The **Festival Internacional del Nuevo Cine Latinoamericano** (festival@icaic.inf.cu) is a major event in all cinemas that should not be missed, see p175. Comprehensive weekly listings of all films from Thursday-Wednesday are posted in cinema windows. Most screenings are at 2000, but the larger cinemas have a showing at around 1700. Observe queuing procedures to buy tickets, mostly 2 pesos or US$2. No drinks or snacks are sold in cinemas but you can take food and drink in with you.

Charles Chaplin, 23 entre 10 y 12, Vedado, **T** 8311101. *Map 4, D11, p253* This is one of the largest art cinemas in Latin America, with modern equipment and film seasons celebrating particular directors, countries or themes. Arty films at 1700 and 2000 with a good shop for memorabilia.

La Rampa, Rampa esquina O, Vedado, **T** 8786146. *Map 3, E6, p250* Shows modern US films and art films from 1630. Nine hundred comfortable seats, but dodgy toilets. There is a nice lobby area with Cuban film posters up the sweeping ramp.

Payret, Prado 503 esquina San José, La Habana Vieja, **T** 8633163. *Map 2, I4, p249* Films shown continuously from 1230 in this very large, popular cinema with fairly comfortable seats. The cinema is quite run down but is a major venue for the film festival.

Riviera, 23 entre Presidentes y H, Vedado, **T** 8309564. *Map 3, E4, p250* The equipment here is unreliable and the a/c often breaks down. US action films are shown. There is a 24-hour snack bar outside.

Yara, opposite *Hotel Habana Libre*, Vedado, **T** 8329430. *Map 3, E5, p250* From 1230, late showings at the weekends on a massive screen. It has comfortable seats although some are broken, 2 video lounges which show recently released US films with 40 seats in each salon. Seats are often sold out at weekends. Dodgy toilets. Snack bar close by.

Dance

Alicia Alonso (1921-) is the most influential Cuban dancer and ballet director, having made her name on the world stage before returning to Cuba to take charge of the development of ballet. The **Ballet Nacional de Cuba** became a showpiece for the revolutionary government and has frequently toured abroad, even to the USA. In Havana it performs at the Teatro García Lorca, with a repertory of classical ballets, folklore-based works and modern dance. Young dancers brought on by the school have a high reputation for their technique and artistic interpretation.

Traditional dances and music are performed by the **Conjunto Folklórico Nacional de Cuba**, Folkcuba, which celebrated its 40th anniversary in 2002. It is dedicated to the survival of the music and dance traditions of Cuba and their African and European roots have been preserved and developed into spectacular theatre performances. The company frequently tours abroad as well as inviting international troupes to perform in Cuba as part of its Folkcuba festivals, see p177. One of its leading lights, choreographer, composer and co-director Rogelio Martínez Furé, won the National Dance Prize in 2002.

There are several contemporary dance companies: **Danza Contemporánea de Cuba** has travelled widely and performs works by numerous choreographers, often drawing on Afrocuban roots and themes; **Danzabierta** uses drama techniques in its dance – the choreography often draws an ironic picture of Cuban reality and the dancers sometimes interact with the audience; **Retazos** puts on grand shows with programmes lasting all night, with influences from the arts such as Lorca's poetry or Fernando Botero's artwork; the **Compañía de la Danza Narciso Medina** is a group of young and highly expressive dancers dedicated to examining the concerns of contemporary Cubans.

Gran Teatro de la Habana, Prado y San José, on Parque Central next to Hotel Inglaterra, **T** 8613078, bic@gth.cult.cu *US$10. Map 2, I4, p249* Opened in 1838, this wonderful baroque building, which seats 1,500 with 2 galleries, has seen countless famous performers on its stage. The Cuban National Ballet and Opera companies perform here in the Sala García Lorca. The Conjunto Folklórico Nacional and Danza Contemporánea dance companies sometimes perform here. It also hosts the International Ballet Festival. Highly recommended.

Teatro Mella, Línea 657 entre A y B, Vedado, **T** 8335651. *8-10 pesos, depending on seat. Map 3, B1, p250* Specializes in modern dance, also with variety shows. The Washington Ballet performed here in 2000 as part of the International Ballet Festival, the first time an American professional ballet company had visited in 40 years. Opus bar on top floor, open 1500-0300, serves light meals, quiet and sophisticated, lift is at opposite end to ground floor café.

Music

Music is the lifeblood of Cuba. Whether it be a street corner rumba or a septeto in the Casa de la Trova, music is everywhere. Cuba's unparalleled musical heritage has spawned the global Pan-Latin musical hysteria, and even the most rigid hipped of north European travellers can't fail to be moved by the Havana's impassioned rhythms. The origins of Cuban music lie in the fusion of a vast cultural gene pool of primarily European, and African cultures, forged by migration, enslavement, war and colonization into a Cuban identity, and forged in the villages and on plantations, in tenements and dockyards. ▸▸ *See also pp224-228.*

Timba "Que sabrosura viva, tremenda expresividad," echoes the chorus, following an opening riff from 'los metales del terror,' surely the scariest horn section ever. La Habana circa 1989 and like

★ **Free entertainment**

Best

• *Azotea de Elda peña*, p135.
• Callejón de Hamel, p68 and p155.
• *Casarón del Tango*, p153.
• *Don Giovanni*, p154.
• El Malecón, p56.

never before, a new band is rocking the city with a tribute to the neighbourhoods. This is not salsa as we've known or might expect it. The structure and feel are fresh and innovative, actually disconcerting. Isn't it jazz or some weird form of rock? You have to pay attention though because this band overflows with virtuosity, breaking tradition consciously, rather than from incompetence. This was NG La Banda, as they said with characteristic modesty, 'la que manda,' a talent concentrate from which some of Cuba's current leading artists emerged to form bands in their own right. The working title of 'Bomba-Son' evolved through the 1990s and onwards with new bands and ideas taking shape from an unprecedented pool of talent. Each has added new ingredients to this urban fusion, lending diversity that defies any categorization that might homogenize it. Today the music has become known loosely as Timba.

Not by chance, the pioneers of NG (new generation) La Banda were drawn largely from two other bands with histories in pushing forward the frontiers of traditional Cuban music. Though not necessarily for dance music, Irakere has been acclaimed internationally for its fusions of jazz with funk, disco, rock and Afro-Cuban rhythm. On the other hand Los Van Van had enjoyed 20 years or so as Cuba's number one dance band, combining elements of pop and pan-Caribbean rhythm within a modernized Charanga band. When some of these two bands' strongest elements got together,

Tango nights
The Casarón del Tango, a shrine to Carlos Gardel, where local legends, including Rafael del Campo (pictured right) brings the audience to tears with sentimental ballads.

then the result was bound to be explosive. The emergence of Timba rests upon the state education system and changing conditions of life no less than upon Cuba's traditions and gifted musicians. These days a musician or arranger's innate talent is complemented with the discipline of a comprehensive academy training. Not that they're stuffed shirts or anything. Timba is streetwise. The symbiotic relationship between the bands and their audience gives inspiration to musicians while elevating to the stage the lives, dreams and preoccupations of Havana's youth. As such, and along with more familiar subjects, songs abound about prostitution, the virtues of soya mince, girlfriends disappeared with rich foreign men and just the struggle to survive. Presented with irony, and the facility of street wit, Timba constitutes an antidote to the escapism of ubiquitous tele-novelas (soap operas). The resulting music is shaking salsa to its foundations.

For those grown accustomed to dancing the predictable structures of Guaracha-Son (the Cuban genre re-named salsa in New York), the hectic shifting of rhythmic patterns so typical of Timba can feel like having the ground drop away from under your feet. Likewise the Rap-derived shouted chorus which appeared in the mid 1990s can jar on your ears at first, the overall sound seeming tuneless and chaotic. Losing your preconceptions of how salsa should be though, you begin to realise that however precarious it seems, Timba is, like a number of things you'll find in Cuba, quite ingeniously stuck together.

Jazz Cuban jazz is exceptionally healthy. Orquesta Irakere continue to renew themselves, inspired by the pianistic genius of Jesús 'Chucho' Valdéz, while Grupo Afro-Cuba fuse jazz with traditional Cuban rhythms, including the bata drums of Santería. Among the generation of the 1980s and 1990s the incredible pianist Gonzalo Rubalcaba is supreme, composing pieces using danzón rhythms amongst others. The annual Jazz Festival in Havana was for years attended by Dizzy Gillespie, whose influence is evident in the playing of Cubans such as Arturo Sandóval and has recently heard British jazzers giving their all.

Rap The Cuban youth, ever more removed from the revolutionary ideals often romantised in 1950s son and Canción Habanero, are increasingly finding a new voice for their millenial angst. In the local Casas de La Cultura across Havana, social comment erupts from a frenetic fusion of latin beats - son, salsa, bolero and cha cha cha, with New York rap. There are now more than 250 rap groups in Cuba, building on Cuba's rich musical heritage and legendary figures such as Beny Moré. Previously muted by the government's radio censorship, rappers now receive the support of Hermanos Saiz, the Youth Communist Union.

While the agenda of 'El Rap' is certainly not to bash outright the ideals of the revolution, street smart lyrics are peppered with messages to the masses of Cuba's underlying problems of racism and sexual discrimination. The group Eddyk is at the forefront of rap's mainstream emergence. The protesting lyrics of band front man Eddy Mora are tame compared to those of Causa 2 who, at the Habana Hip Hop festival 2002, lampooned the state-owned media for their discriminatory enforcement of Cuban racial stereotyping and tropical tourist apartheid.

▸▸ *For music venues see Bars and clubs, p145.*

Theatre

Drama, opera, classical concerts and fringe theatre can all be found, although you should be aware that all works are in Spanish. Theatres mushroomed in the 19th century when Havana attracted artists from all over the world. After the Revolution, the **Teatro Nacional** was founded, which gave theatre a boost. Between 1959 and 1961 124 new plays were staged. Virgilio Piñera was one of the leading playwrights of the 20th century, but during the 1960s other names proliferated, such as José Brene, Héctor Quintero, Antón Arrufat, Nicolás Dorr and Carlos Felipe. Experimentation was the order of the day, notably for the **Teatro Escambray**, which took theatre out into the countryside for a *campesino* audience. Other companies were the **Teatro Estudio**, **Teatro Político Bertold Brecht** and the **Grupo Rita Montaner**.

Drama festivals were started in the 1980s and have been impor-tant in introducing ideas from visiting international theatre companies. There are many small drama companies struggling to put on performances with limited funds for costumes, scenery and props, but the acting and direction are faultless. Look out for theatre groups such as **Teatro Obstáculo** (La Cuarta Pared, Opera Ciega, Segismundo ex-marqués, El Arca), **Teatro Irrumpe** (Dos Viejos Pánicos, La Noche), **Teatro el Público** (Té y simpatía, El Público, Calígula), Teatro Mío (Manteca, Delirio Habanero) and **Buendía** (La Cándida Eréndira, Las Ruinas Circulares, Roberto Zucco). Plays range from European classics to avant-garde or worthy revolutionary material, but contemporary works are not above having a dig at current social problems.

The **Orquesta Sinfonía Nacional** is probably the best in the Caribbean, but all classical musicians in Cuba are hindered by a lack of decent instruments. International orchestras frequently play in Havana and you can see some excellent, world-famous musicians for a pittance. *Amistur* travel agency, see p211, can help with theatre bookings.

Amadeo Roldán, Calzada y D, Vedado, **T** 8321168. *Map 3, B2, p250* Fabulously renovated concert hall, Sala Caturla, where you can hear the *Orquesta Sinfónica Nacional* and visiting international symphony orchestras, including several from the USA. Pay in pesos.

Gran Teatro de la Habana, Prado y San José, on Parque Central next to *Hotel Inglaterra*, **T** 8613078, bic@gth.cult.cu *US$10. Map 2, I4, p249* As well as ballet in the García Lorca auditorium (see Dance), there is drama in the Antonín Artaud and Alejo Carpentier studio theatres.

Teatro Karl Marx, Av 1 entre 8 y 10, Miramar, **T** 230801/ 291991. *Map 4, A7, p253* Renovated in 2000 and now famous for hosting the first rock concert by a Western band, Manic Street Preachers, who played here in 2001 in the presence of Fidel Castro.

Teatro Nacional de Cuba, Paseo y 39, Vedado, **T** 8335713.
Map 3, J1, p251 Quite an entertainment centre this, with lots going on all the time. Downstairs in the theatre there are live concerts such as a Nueva Trova shows for 10 pesos. There is a piano bar *El Delirio Habanero*, see p157, and club, *Café Cantante*, in the basement, see p156.

Sala Hubert de Blanck, Calzada entre A y B, Vedado, **T** 8335962. *Map 3, B1, p250* Specializes in classical and contemporary music concerts, but has also staged major works by García Lorca and Cuban playwright Abelardo Estorino, as well as contemporary dance companies, Danzabierta and Danza Contemporánea.

Teatro El Sótano, K entre 25 y 27, Vedado, **T** 8320630.
Map 3, E5, p250 Shows contemporary drama, somewhere to find fringe theatre and home of the Rita Montaner Company.

Teatro Trianón, Línea entre Paseo y A, Vedado, **T** 8309648.
Map 3, B1, p250 Part cinema, part theatre. It is small and in good condition. The seats have quirky pull-out extensions for you to rest your thighs on!

Teatro Guiñol, M entre 19 y 21, Vedado, **T** 8326262.
Map 3, D6, p250 Children's theatre specializing in marionettes.

The year in Havana is crammed with festivals. The most popular events are the cinema and jazz festivals, but there are ballet and contemporary dance festivals as well as celebrations of folk music, classical music, guitar and boleros, etc. There are no national religious festivals, although you will find some patron saints' days celebrated (often linked to Santería) and Easter is an important time.

Public holidays commemorate political and historical events and are marked by rallies in the Plaza de la Revolución. Carnival has been resurrected, although it is not held at the traditional pre-Lenten time. Parades and competitions take place over several weekends in the summer instead.

Contact the *Buró de Convenciones*, Edif Focsa, Calle M entre 17 y 19, Vedado, T 8313600, F 8334261, www.buroconv.cubaweb.cu It publishes an events list with contacts. Music and dance festivals are organized by the agency, *Paradiso*, icm@artsoft.cult.cu or uneac@artsoft.cult.cu, while fishing tournaments are arranged by *Cubatur*. Contact Juan M Caibo Pérez, T 8782842, F 8335408.

January

New Year is celebrated with great fanfare, largely because it coincides with Liberation Day, marking the end of the Batista dictatorship, on 1 January 1959. There is lots of music and dancing, and general merriment, washed down with copious quantities of rum.

 Cuballet de Invierno (6 January-2 February 2003), **Folkcuba** and **Cubadanza** (6-17 January 2003) are twice-yearly dance festivals. For Cuballet de Invierno contact Laura Alonso, of Prodanza, T 2608610, prodanza@cubarte.cult.cu; for Folkcuba, the Conjunto Folklórico Nacional de Cuba, Juan García, T 8334560, cnae@min.cult.cu; Cubadanza, Cuban Contemporary Dance, Miguel Iglesias, T 8796410, cnae@min.cult.cu

February

The **Havana International Book Fair** (31 January -9 February 2003) is held at El Morro – a commercial fair in new, purpose-built convention buildings. Look out for new book launches. Pedro Pérez Sarduy launched his novel, *The Maids of Havana*, there in 2002. Contact Sr Iroel Sánchez, T 8624739, iroel@icl.cult.cu

The **Cigar Festival,** introduced in the last few years, is for true aficionados of *Habanos*. Held 24-28 February at the Palacio de las Convenciones, you can learn about the history of cigars and there are opportunities for visits to tobacco plantations and cigar factories. Contact Ana López, T 2040513, Alopez@habanos.cu

March

Spring in Havana, International Electrical Acoustic Music Festival, in the last week of the month, with workshops and performances. Contact Juan Blanco, T 8303983, inmc@cubarte.cult.cu

April

International Percussion Festival 'PERCUBA' (15-19 April 2003), for a week in the middle of the month at the Teatro Nacional. Percuba (Percussion Society of Cuba) organizes a programme of theoretical and practical events and competitions to promote percussion at home and abroad. Contact Lino Arturo Neira Betancourt, T 2038808, lneira@cubarte.cult.cu

Cuba Pista Cycling Cup, in the second week, for track racing competitions. Cyclists everywhere and a popular event with habaneros. Contact Alberto Puig,T 2040945, gral@inder.co.cu

May

May Theatre at the Casa de las Américas in the second week, with workshops and performances. Contact Vivian Martínez Tabares, T 552706, teatro@casa.cult.cu

Havana International Guitar Festival and Competition, also in the second week, with performers and competitors from around the world. Contact Vivian Martínez Tabares, T 552706, teatro@casa.cult.cu

June

International Ernest Hemingway White Marlin Fishing Tournament (9-14 June 2003) is held at the beginning of the month at the Marina Hemingway. Contact José Miguel Díaz Escrich, T 2041689, yachtclub@cnih.mh.cyt.cu

International Boleros de Oro Festival (22-29 June 2003) for aficionados of boleros. Contact Dr José Loyola Fernández, T 8320395, promocion@uneac.co.cu

July

Folkcuba workshop in the first two weeks, **Cubadanza** (1-12 July 2003) and **Cuballet de Verano** (7 July-3 August 2003), are summer dance festivals, see January.

Carnival is held at weekends between mid-July and mid-August, with parades along the Malecón, competitions, and lots of partying with drumming, singing and dancing. Contact Francisco Cairo Silva, T 8323742, atic@cubarte.cult.cu

Que Siempre Brille el Sol baseball tournament (25-30 September 2003), always a popular event in this baseball-mad country. Contact Alberto Puig, T 2040945, gral@cubadeportes.cu

September

International Blue Marlin Fishing Tournament (8-13 September 2003), at the Marina Hemingway. Not much of a spectator sport but the marina fills up with mostly US fishermen eager to pit their strength against marlin and their fellow competitors, with lots of après-fishing social events. Contact José Miguel Díaz Escrich, T 2041689, yachtclub@cnih.mh.cyt.cu

October

Havana Contemporary Music Festival (1-9 October 2003), usually runs for nine days at the start of the month in theatres and UNEAC. Contact Guido López Gavilán, T 8320194, musicos@uneac.co.cu

Havana International Ballet Festival (19-28 October 2002), at the Gran Teatro, is run by Alicia Alonso, head of the Cuban National Ballet,T 552948, bnc@cubarte.cult.cu

November

International Festival of University Theatre (25-30 November 2002) is held in theatres in the last week, showcasing student drama. Contact Reynaldo González López, T 552356, extuniv@reduniv.edu.cu

December

International Festival of New Latin American Cinema. Shows prize-winning films (no subtitles) at cinemas around Havana in the first two weeks of the month (3-13 December 2002 and 2003). This is the foremost film festival in Latin America with the best of Cuban and Latin American films along with documentaries and independent cinema from Europe and the USA. See the stars as well as the films, as the festival attracts big-name actors and producers. Contact Alfredo Guevara, head of the Cuban Institute of Cinematographic Art and Industry (ICAIC), T 552854, presidenciafestival@icaic.inf.cu, www.habanafilmfestival.com

International Jazz Plaza Festival (13-17 December 2002) at theatres and the Casa de la Cultura de Plaza. This follows the film festival, running into the third week of December, and is a great time to overload on music and cinema. It is one of the world's major jazz festivals with the best of Cuban and international jazz. There are masterclasses and workshops available and the event is organized by Grammy winner Jesús 'Chucho' Valdés, T 8321234, icm@cubarte.cult.cu

Happy End of Year Regatta, at Marina Hemingway for three days up to New Year, with social events that always accompany the racing fraternity. Contact José Miguel Díaz Escrich, T 2041689, cnih@cbcan.cyt.cu

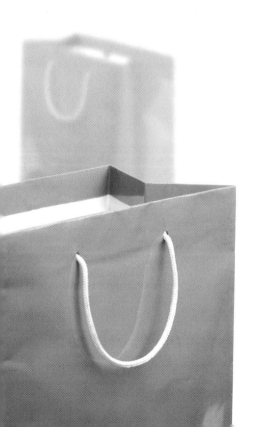

Shopping

Havana is not a great shopping experience and you will not find trendy areas with designer boutiques. The US trade embargo and lack of foreign exchange means imports are often in short supply although shops are improving. The main souvenirs to take home have to be rum, cigars and maybe coffee. *Caracol* shops in hotels and in La Habana Vieja and Vedado sell tourist items, rum and cigars. Cigars can often be seen being made in hotel lobbies or cigar lounges, where you can also buy them. Handicrafts are being developed for tourists and markets in La Habana Vieja and Vedado hold an overwhelming amount of stock as Cubans cash in on the chance to earn dollars. There is a considerable amount of art of varying degrees of worth, but you may pick up a bargain. If you are a serious collector, go straight to the galleries. Taking art out of the country requires a special licence; galleries and vendors in the market can give you the necessary stamp. There are no delis stocking Cuban specialities, but farmers' markets, *agromercados*, sell delicious tropical fruits and vegetables in season at rock bottom prices in pesos.

Havana

Music

Casa de la Música EGREM shop, 20 esquina 35, Miramar, **T** 2040447. *1000-2430. Map 4, E5, p252* Well stocked with good selection of CDs/music.

Artex, L esquina 23, Vedado, **T** 8320632. *Mon-Sat 0900-2100, Sun 1000-1600, directions. Map 3, E5, p250* Has an excellent music section.

Art galleries

Estudio Acella, Oficios 18a entre Obrapía y Obispo, next door to Casa de los Arabes. *Map 6, D4, p256* At the tiny studio of Blanca Acella Escalante you can buy affordable figurative canvases inspired by this popular *habanera*'s travels through Italy, Spain and Mexico.

Estudio Galería Rigoberto Mena, see p43. *Map 6, D3, p256* Rigoberto is one of Cuba's hottest contemporary artists.

Galería del Grabado, at the back of the *Taller Experimental de Gráfica de la Habana*, Callejón del Chorro 62, Plaza de la Catedral, **T** 620979, **F** 338121. *Open all day, closed Sun. Map 6, C3, p256* You can watch the prints and engravings being made and specialist courses are available for those who want to learn the skill for themselves, for 1 month, US$250, or 3 months, US$500.

Galería Los Oficios, see p48. *Map 6, F4, p256* Gallery of Nelsón Domínguez, one of Cuba's most prolific contemporary Cuban artists.

► Buying cigars

On the street, cigars are bound to be fakes, no matter how good a deal they appear. Check the quality of each cigar. They should be tightly rolled, not soft; they should have no lumps or other protuberances; if you turn them upside down nothing should come out; the colour should be uniform and the aroma should be strong. The box should be sealed with the four-language warranty, which should not be a photocopy, and on the bottom you should find the stamp: "Habanos s.a. HECHO EN CUBA Totalmente a mano. "

You may take only 50 cigars out of the country without a receipt, but if you buy them in a state shop and get a valid receipt you can buy cigars up to a value of US$2,000 (unless you are returning to the USA, where the embargo forbids you to import Cuban cigars of any worth).

Cigars are like fine wines or whiskies and there are many different types from which to choose. Castro used to smoke *Cohiba* cigars, which were created in 1966 exclusively for the diplomatic market. In 1982 the *Cohiba Lanceros*, *Coronas Especiales* and *Panatelas* were created for public sale, followed in 1989 by the *Espléndidos*, *Robustos* and *Exquisitos*, which together make up the Classic Line (*La Línea Clásica*).

In 1992, to mark the 500th anniversary of the landing of Columbus, the government brought out the 1492 Line (*La Línea 1492*), with its five centuries: Siglo I, II, III, IV, V. The *Espléndidos* now sell for up to US$383 a box. As well as the *Cohiba* brand, there are *Montecristo*, *Romeo y Julieta*, *Bolívar*, *Punch*, *Hoyo de Monterrey*, *H Upmann*, *Partagás*, *Quintero*, *La Flor de Cano*, *El Rey del Mundo* and *Rafael González*, all of which have their company histories and logos, mostly dating from the 19th century.

La Acacia, San José 114 entre Industria y Consulado, Centro, T 613533. *Map 2, I3, p249* This leading gallery provides a showcase for the work of local artists, who have received international acclaim. The work of Nelsón Domínguez and Fabelo appears on the hot list of many an American collector in search of a good investment, but originals still don't come cheap.

Cigars

Casa del Habano, 5 1407 esquina 16, Miramar, **T** 2041185. *Mon-Sat 1030-1830. Map 4, B6, p252* Full range of cigars. This is one of many branches of state cigar shops. Cigars can cost whatever you are prepared to pay, but make sure you buy the best to take home and don't get tricked into buying fakes, as you may not get them through customs.

Casa del Habano Partagás, Industria 520 entre Dragones y Barcelona, behind the Capitolio, **T** 338060. *Daily 0800-1800. Map 2, I3, p249* Shop attached to cigar factory, several brand names made here, tours available every 15 mins, 0930-1500, US$10.

Rum

Fundación Distilería Havana Club, Av del Puerto 262 entre Sol y Muralla, **T** 618051. *Daily 0900-1700. Map 6, H4, p256* Havana Club shop attached to the Rum Museum.

La Casa del Tabaco y Ron, Obispo esquina Monserrate, La Habana Vieja. *Mon-Sat 0900-1700. Map 2, I4, p249* Displaying a wide range of rums of all ages and tobacco. The street price of a bottle of rum ranges from US$2-4 for poor quality to US$4-8 for a five-year-old rum.

Shopping

★ Ways to blow the budget

Best

- An eighth floor suite at the *Hotel Nacional*, p140.
- Lobster at *Tococoro*, p143.
- A stock of *Cohiba* cigars, Fidel's choice, p184.
- Duty free allowance of *Havana Club San Cristóbal* special reserve, p185.
- Going Bogart, with cocktails at *El Floridita*, p127 and p149.

Food markets

Agromercados, farmers' markets, in Vedado at 19 y B. *Map 3, D1, p250*. A smaller one at 21 esquina J. *Map 3, D4, p250* In Centro, the Chinese market at the junction of Zanja and Av Italia. *Map 2, H2, p249* You can eat at street food stalls (avoid Monday, not a good day). *Cadeca* exchange bureaux at the first and last listed. The last Sunday of every month there is a large food market held in Paseo, between Calzada de Zapata and the *Teatro Nacional*. *Map ref: p234 G4*. Good value and lots of produce, oranges 10 centavos each, a hand of green bananas 2 pesos.

Handicrafts

Feria del Malecón, Malecón, entre D y E, Vedado. *Thu-Tue 0800-1830*. *Map 3, A2, p250*

Feria del Tacón, Av Tacón entre Chacón y Empedrado, La Habana Vieja, Plaza de la Catedral end *Wed-Mon 0800-1900*. *Map 2, H7, p249*. Both very busy markets, the latter is the larger. Inlaid wooden boxes for cigars, jewellery, baseball bats, model sailing ships, ceramics, Santería items, Che Guevara hats and innumerable T-shirts for sale. Do not buy black coral or tortoiseshell as these are protected species and it will probably be illegal to take it in to your own country.

Pelota (baseball) is Cuba's national pastime. In Havana's back streets kids hone their skills from an early age, and the older generation's match post mortems reach fever pitch in Parque Central. The season runs from October-May, culminating in the national play-offs. Sport plays an important part in stimulating national pride. Cuba's amateur athletes, supported and trained by the state, enjoy an elite, quasi-professional status. Olympic gold medallists, including boxing legend Teófilo Stevenson, join the pantheon of Cuba's national heroes. In 1991, Cuba hosted the Pan-American Games. Amassing 140 gold medals, Fidel and the nation revelled in its victory over the USA, a first for any Latin nation. In the 2000 Olympic Games in Sydney, Cuba's medal haul totalled 27, finishing in eighth place – a great achievement for a hard-pressed country with a population of 11 million. There are plenty of activities, which provide opportunities to explore beyond the city. Riding and cycling are very popular, and you can reach the Playas del Este beaches and surrounding countryside easily.

Havana

Baseball

Estadio Latinoamericano, Zequeira 312, (Pedro Pérez), Cerro, **T** 706576. *Games at 1930 Tue-Thu and Sat, Oct-May. 3 pesos. Map 3, L2, p251* The best place to see major league baseball. Opened in the 1950s, it has a capacity for 55,000 spectators and is home to the Havana teams, Industriales (Los Azules) and Metropolitanos.

Basketball

Estadio Ramón Fonst, Av Independencia y Bruzón, Plaza de la Revolución, **T** 820000. *Map 3, J1, p251* Basketball season runs from September-November. The local team is Capitalinos.

Boxing

Sala Kid Chocolate, Paseo de Martí y Brasil, La Habana Vieja, **T** 611547. *US$3. Map 2, I4, p249* Cuba's boxing skills are internationally recognised. Although Cuba finished top in the 2000 Olympics' boxing tournament with four gold medals, Castro still launched a scathing attack against "a disgusting mafia" of judges, which he claimed had "robbed" Yosvany Aguilera and Juan Hernández Sierra of medals.

Cycling

Blazing Saddles Travels, saddles100@aol.com or info@cyclecuba.net Mountain bikes can be hired at US$5 per day, puncture repair kits and spare inner tubes are provided. See also Directory, p201.

Golf

Club de Golf, Carretera de Vento, Km 8, Capdevila, Boyeros, towards the airport, **T** 558746, gere@clgolf.ch.cubalse.cu *US$5 golf club hire, US$30 for 18 holes. Map 1, p247* There is also a miniature bowling alley, billiards (3 tables), tennis (bring your own rackets), squash and grubby pool, US$5 including a drink, a bar and a poor restaurant/snack bar, *La Estancia*.

Horse riding

El Rodeo, Parque Lenín. *US$5 per hr, including guide. Map 1, p247* It is mostly for Cubans and you may be able to pay in pesos. No reservations, just turn up. The horses are well cared for.

Stadiums

Ciudad Deportiva, Av Boyeros y Vía Blanca. *Camello M3 and M2 and bus P2 pass outside. 2 pesos for seats and 1 peso for concrete benches in upper tiers.* Buy tickets in advance at the venue; international matches are usually a sell out. Volleyball, basketball, martial arts, table tennis. Great atmosphere, crowded and limited food and drink facilities.

Swimming pools

Hotel Nacional, Calle O esquina 21, Vedado, **T** 3335647. *US$15 consumo mínimo, pool side bar or US$20 including lunchtime buffet. Map 3, D7, p250* Chill out and unwind with great views over the Malecón, lovely pool, comfy sun loungers, towels provided.

Parque Lenín, Calle 100 y Cortina de la Presa, Arroyo Naranjo. *Free. Map 1, p247* Open-air pools, see p96.

Watersports

Centro de Buceo La Aguja, *Club Habana (Sol Meliá)*, Av 5 188-192, Reparto Flores, Playa, **T** 2045700, **F** 2045705. *US$15 for a daily membership.* The dive centre takes up to 8 divers on the boat. *Club Habana* runs the rest of the watersports.

Club Habana (Sol Meliá), Av 5 entre 188 y 192, Playa, **T** 2045700/2043301-4. The main house dates back to 1928 and was the Havana Biltmore Yacht and Country Club. It is very posh but has lots of facilities on land and in the water. Tennis, squash, pool, sailing, motor boats, diving, windsurfing, training golf course, child care, shops, meetings facilities, sauna and massage, bar and restaurant, expensive.

Around Havana

Watersports and recreation centre

Club Náutico Internacional 'Hemingway', Marina Hemingway, Av 5 y 248, Playa, **T/F** 2041689/2046653. *20 mins by taxi (US$10-15) from Havana.* *Map 1, p247* A social club for foreign executives based in Cuba. The notice board is a good place to find crewing opportunities. The club organizes regattas, sailing schools and excursions, as well as the Hemingway Tournament.

! At the Sydney Olympics, Cuba took the gold medal for sexual stamina, getting through the highest number of the free 25,000 condoms provided to athletes at the Olympic village. It also did some losing along the way with dozens of defectors heading for the free world during the 2000 games including baseball all stars Livan and Orlando `El Duque' Hernández pitching off for the Giants and the Yankees.

Marlin 'Marina Hemingway', Marina Hemingway, Av 5 y 248, Playa, **T** 2041150-57, **F** 2041149. *Mon-Fri 0800-1700. Map 1, p247* Boat trips, sport fishing, US$450 half day, motorized sports, catamarans, sailing, windsurfing, diving and snorkelling.

Mi Cayito Recreation Centre, Av de las Terrazas, Laguna Itabo, Santa María, near Boca Ciega, Playas del Este, **T** 971339. *1000-1800. Map 5, A9, p255* Equipment for hire includes a catamaran (US$10 per hr, up to five people), a fast launch with a driver (US$20 per 20 mins, up to six people) for a nature tour of the channels, a pedal boat (US$1.50 per hr) with four seats. Showers and changing rooms available. Motorcycle rentals at an inland lake.

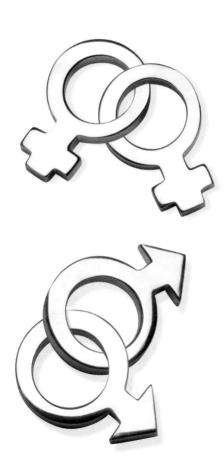

Cuba's brand of *machismo* and the hallowed image of the beret-clad revolutionary who is all man created a notoriously homophobic society. Following the Revolution, homosexuality was denounced by Fidel as "a bourgeois perversion" and *maricones* were sent to hard labour camps to be "rehabilitated". The 1980 Mariel exodus was characterized as the flight of criminals, mental patients and homosexuals. Some 125,000 Cubans were aided by their US-based compatriots who took boats over to meet them when restrictions on leaving were lifted by Castro.

In the latter part of the 1980s attitudes changed as Castro sought allies from more liberal regimes. The film, *Fresa y Chocolate,* stimulated much debate and brought about the end of the quarantine of HIV patients. Although Cuba is still a macho society, there is more tolerance of gay people, and gay travellers will not generally encounter any problems. However, the Cuban Association for Gays and Lesbians, formed in 1994, operated until 1997 when it was finally suppressed by the government. There are no laws against homosexuality and assaults are rare.

Nightlife

There are no state bars and clubs, or gay and lesbian scene, as such, in Havana. In August 1999, the well-known gay disco *El Periquito* was the scene of a government crackdown, with over 600 gay people fined and threatened with imprisonment.

Entertainment and nightlife now principally centres around private parties. The location of where the action takes place is not so discreetly communicated at 2200 in front of the Yara cinema on La Rampa.

Entertainment can include anything from drag queens to techno rave. Charges are usually in pesos although you may be expected to pay in dollars, usually around US$1.

For an excellent account of Cuban attitudes to homosexuals, see *Machos, Maricones and Gays, Cuba and Homosexuality*, in Books, p222. From the world of film, see *Antes que Anochezca* and *Fresa y Chocolate*, see p222 .

Havana

Gay friendly casas particulares

Jesús y María, La Habana Vieja. Self-contained rooms and a tranquil, leafy interior courtyard, see p105. *Map 2, K5, p249*

Villa Colonial Tomy, Centro. Multicoloured rooms in a casa particular run by a ballet teacher extraordinaire, see p114. *Map 2, F1, p248*

Jorge Coallo Potts, Vedado. Great conversation in this conveniently located casa particular, see p117. *Map 3, D5, p250*

Gay friendly paladares

La Guarida, Centro. An appearance in the movie *Fresa y Chocolate* cemented the reputation of this recommended paladar serving up tantalising delights, see p133. *Map 2, F1, p248*

La Tasquita, Centro. Delicious home cooking served up with panache amid festive chintz plus rocking cocktails to kick-start the evening, see p133. *Map 3, F7, p250*

Le Chansonnier, Vedado. Great conversation at this pastel pink paladar. Silver service dining and bountiful platters of fruit and veg, see p136. *Map 3, C4, p250*

La Cocina de Liliam, Miramar. Always book ahead at this stylish paladar which serves mouth-watering cooking in a pre-Raphaelite courtyard setting. From here, taxi down to *El Tropical*, see p141, for a flamboyant disco and the hottest live salsa in town, see p141. *Map 4, D2, p252*

La Esperanza, Miramar. For the Almodóvar experience and Parisien food flair, the hosts of La Esperanza, will also keep you from the edge of a nervous breakdown by propping your evening up with potent mango daiquiris, see p142. *Map 4, A6, p252*

Havana is not really a city for small children, who tend to get bored sightseeing, and it is not easy to push a buggy, with high pavements and lots of pot holes and loose paving stones. However, Cubans love kids and restaurants are child friendly. There are no international fast food chains but *El Rápido* and *Burgui* sell burgers or chicken and chips, and pizza and pasta are available. Some *casas particulares* offer kitchen facilities or will cook for you, so you can make sure your children get a nutritious meal. Many rooms in private houses sleep three or four people. They are unlikely to have cots, but families are usually very willing to babysit for a small fee. Hotels also organize baby sitting services. Take baby food, nappies/diapers, wet wipes, toilet paper, books and toys. There are zoos and amusement parks for the younger ones, but the 10-12 age range would be better entertained with excursions to Parque Lenín or further afield. The beach is never far away. Teenagers will appreciate the music and dance, with opportunities to meet young Cubans at afternoon or early evening events.

Havana

Museums

Museo Nacional de Historia Natural, Plaza de Armas, Obispo 61, **T** 8632687, museo@mnhnc.inf.cu *Tue-Fri 0930-1730, Sat and Sun 0930-1630. US$3.* Written information is in Spanish only. *Map 6, D5 p256   See also p36.* This museum has hundreds of stuffed species - endemic to Cuba and around the world and will keep kids fascinated for some hours.

Museo de Naipes, Plaza Vieja, Muralla 101, **T** 8601534. *Tue-Sat 0900-1445, Sun 0900-1300.* Donations welcome. *Map 6, G2, p256 See also p53.* Plenty of colourful cards to amuse the kids.

Music and dance

Casa de la Música, 20 esquina 35, Miramar, **T** 2040447. *1000-0300.   Map 4, E5, p252 See also p160.*   Daily afternoon live music sessions, *peñas*, 1600-1900, 10-15 pesos, suitable for young teenagers.

El Tropical, Salón Rosado Beny Moré, Av 41 y 46, Miramar, **T** 290985. *Sun afternoons.   Map 4, G5, p252 See also p161.* 'Third age' salsa activity outdoors on Sunday afternoons, very popular, mostly Cuban crowd.

Café Cantante Mi Habana, Teatro Nacional, Paseo y 39, Vedado, **T** 8335713. *1600-1900.   Map 3, J1, p251 See also p156.*   Popular salsa and rock discos, *Tardes de mi Habana*, sometimes with live bands, 10 pesos.

Kids

Parks and zoos

Parque Lenín, north of Rancho Boyeros, near the airport. *Map 1, p247 See also p96.* A large park with boating lake and horse riding. Popular with Cuban families at weekends. Aquarium with fresh water fish.

Parque Zoológico Nacional, Km 3, Carretera de Capdevila, **T** 447613. *Tue-Sun 0930-1530. US$3 adults, US$2 children. Map 1, p247 See also p97.* Over 900 animals and 100 different species. Also has an interactive children's zoo with small animals and pony rides.

Acuario, Calle 62 y Av 3, Miramar, **T** 2036401, acuario@ama.cu *Tue-Sun 1000-1800. Map 4, B1, p252 See also p87.* Salt water creatures and dolphinarium. Interactive displays.

La Maestranza, Parque Céspedes, Av del Puerto, La Habana Vieja, **T** 6227979. *Wed-Sun 1000-2000. Entrance 20 centavos; 50 centavos per ride. Map 6, B5, p256. Amusement park suitable for toddlers-8 years.*

Airline offices

Air Europa, Hotel Habana Libre, T 666918-9. Mon-Fri 0900-1330, 1430-1800, Sat 0900-1300. **Air France**, Hotel Habana Libre, T 662644/662642. Mon-Fri 0830-1200, 1300-1630, Sat 0830-1230. **Air Jamaica**, Hotel Meliá Cohiba, T 662447/333636, F 662449. At airport: T 330212. **Cubana**. For international sales: 23 64, esquina Infanta, T 334469/334950. For national sales: Infanta esquina Humboldt, T 706714. **Iberia**, 23 74 esquina P, very busy, take ticket and wait your turn, T 335041-2, 335064, F335061. At the airport: T 335234. **LTU**, 23 64 esquina Infanta, T 333524-5, F 333590. **Martinair Holland,** 23 esquina P, T 334364/333730, F 333729. **Mexicana de Aviación**, 23 64 esquina P, T 333531-2, F 333077.

Banks and ATMs

For dollar services, credit card withdrawals, TCs and exchange:
Banco Financiero Internacional, Línea esquina O, Vedado, T 333003/333148, F 333006. Mon-Fri 0800-1500, last day of the month until 1200; a branch in *Hotel Habana Libre*, T 333429, F 333795, same opening times; Teniente Rey esquina Oficios, La Habana Vieja; and 18 111 entre 1 y 3, Miramar, T 332058, F 332458. **Banco Internacional de Comercio**, 20 de Mayo y Ayestarán, Plaza de la Revolución, Vedado, T 555482-5. Mon-Fri 0830-1400. **Banco Metropolitano**, Línea 63 esquina M, Vedado, T 553116-8. Mon-Sat 0830-1500. **Buró de Turismo**, *Hotel Habana Libre*, gives credit card cash advances. Mon-Fri 0900-1700.
Exchange bureau in *Hotel Nacional* offers credit card cash advances. Mon-Sat 0800-1200, 1230-1930. A Visa ATM in the lobby of the *Hotel Parque Central* issues convertible pesos to a certain limit, but it is not always working. There is also an ATM in the Plaza Carlos III shopping centre, Av Salvador Allende, but again, it only issues pesos convertibles. Credit card advances from exchange houses, *cadecas*, incur a standard 1.5% handling charge. The *Cadeca* on Obispo y Compostela is open until 2200. Banks are not open on Christmas Day, New Year's Day or Sundays.

Bicycle hire

Blazing Saddles Travels rents out mountain bikes at US$15 per day, provides puncture repair kits and spare inner tubes. Contact saddles100@aol.com, info@cyclecuba.net Bikes and scooters can be hired at Av 3 entre 28 y 30, Miramar. **Cubalinda** hires touring bikes (Peugeot or Norco) for US$11 per day, less for longer, from Edif Someillan, O 2 entre Línea y 17, Piso 27, Vedado, T 553980, reservations@cubalinda.com

Car hire

Through state rental companies at the International Airport and most large hotels, www.dtcuba.com/esp/transporte_tierra.asp or try the companies direct. **Cubacar**, 1 16401, Miramar, T 332277, F 330760, pmando@cubacar.cha.cyt.cu **Havanautos**, 1 esquina O, Edif Sierra Maestra, Miramar, T 2039658, F 2040648, www.havanautos.cu **Transtur**, Cuba 60, Piso 9, La Habana Vieja, T 8616788, F 8615885, www.transtur.cu **Vía Rent a Car**, Av del Puerto 102 entre Obrapía y Jústiz, T 8614465/339781, F 331879; Av 100 y 31, Playa, T 204455, res_rc@gaviota.gav.tur.cu

Credit card lines

See Travel Essentials, p19. **Asistur**, see p205, can help in emergencies.

Disabled
Cubanacán Turismo y Salud,

www.cubanacan.cu/turismo/salud runs health tourism with specialized hotels/hospitals for people with specific needs such as physiotherapy, kidney dialysis or other treatment, but outside these centres there are few facilities for disabled people. New hotels have been built with a couple of rooms adapted for people using wheelchairs, but the older hotels usually have no facilities and neither do casas particulares. In the latter, make sure you can have a ground floor room and that passages and doorways are negotiable with wheels. It is advisable to book in advance with a good tour company who can ensure that the correct transport is available for transfers and excursions. Havana is not wheelchair-friendly. Pavements are usually built up much higher than the roads, which makes crossing the road hazardous for anyone with mobility difficulties. Potholes and loose paving stones compound the difficulties.

Electricity
110 Volts, 3 phase 60 cycles, AC. Plugs are usually of the American type. In some new tourist hotel developments, however, European plugs are used, with 220 volts, although they often provide adaptors. Check in advance if it is important to you.

Embassies
All in Miramar unless stated otherwise: **Austria**, Calle 4 101, esquina Av 1, T 2042825, F 2041235. Mon-Fri 0900-1200. **Belgium**, Av 5 7408 esquina 76, T 2042410, F 2041318. Mon-Fri 0900-1200. **Canada**, 30 518 esquina 7, T 2042516, F 2041069. Mon, Tue, Thu, Fri 0830-1700, Wed 0830-1400. **Czech Republic**, Av Kohly 259 entre 41 y 43, Nuevo Vedado, T 333467. Tue-Fri 0900-1200. **France**, 14 312 entre 3 y 5, T 2042132, F 2041439. Mon-Fri 0830-1230. **Germany**, B 652 esquina 13, Vedado, T 332569, F 331586. Mon-Fri 0900-1200. **Italy**, Paseo 606 entre 25 y 27, Vedado, T 333334, F 333416. Visas Tue and Fri 1030-1300. **Japan**, 3 y 80, Centro de Negocios, 5th floor, T 2043508, F2048902, Mon-Fri 0900-1500. **Netherlands**, 8 307 entre 3 y 5, T 2042511/2, F 2042059. Mon-Fri 0830-1130. **Russia**, 5 6402 entre 62 y 66, T 2042686, F 2041038. Mon-Fri 0800-1200, 1500-1800. **Portugal**, 7 2207, esquina 24, T 2042871, F 2012593. Mon-Fri 0900-1230. **South Africa**, 5 4201 esquina 42, T 2049671-6, F 2041101. Mon-Fri 0900-1200. **Spain**, Cárcel 51 esquina Zulueta, La Habana Vieja, T 338025/338026, F 338006. Mon-Fri 0800-1530. **Sweden**, 34 510 entre 5 y 7, T 2042831/2042971,

ambassaden.havanna@foreign.ministry.se Mon-Fri 0900-1200.
Switzerland, Av 5 2005, T 2042611, F 2041148. Mon-Fri
0900-1300. **UK**, 34 702 y 704, T 2041771, F 2048104,
embrit@ceniai.inf.cu Commercial Section open Mon-Fri
0800-1530. The **US Interests Section** of the Swiss Embassy,
Calzada entre L y M, Vedado, T 333551/334401.

Emergency numbers
Police: T 820116. **Fire**: T 811115/798561-69.
Asistur, linked to overseas insurance companies, can help with
emergency hospital treatment, repatriations, robbery, direct trans-
fer of funds to Cuba, financial and legal problems, travel insurance
claims etc. For (24-hour) emergencies go to Paseo Martí 212 entre
Trocadero y Colón, La Habana Vieja, T 338527/338920/571314-5,
F 338087, asisten@asisten.get.cma.net Commercial office in
Miramar, Calle 4 110 entre 1 y 3, T 2048835, F 2048088,
www.asistur.cubaweb.cu

Internet/email
Internet access is available at a limited number of places: Inside the
Capitolio. There are nine terminals, US$3 for 30 mins, US$5 per hr,
open 0800-1800 (although 2000 is advertized but the Capitolio is
shut by then). You may have to wait up to 45 mins for one to be
free. The large hotels of 4 or 5 stars, such as the *Habana Libre*,
Nacional, *Parque Central*, *Meliá Cohiba*, all have business centres
with computers for internet access, as well as telephone, fax and
telex facilities, but they charge a lot more, eg US$5 for 30 mins at
the *Nacional* and US$7 for 30 mins at the *Parque Central* (business
centre on 1st floor, ext 1911/1833, open 0800-2000). The best
value and most convenient facilities are in the bar of the *Hotel
Telégrafo* on Parque Central, US$2.50 per 30 mins, US$5 per hr.
There are often queues, but the bar serves great daiquiris to ease
the wait. The *Hotel Plaza*, Parque Central, also has internet facilities
at US$6 per hr. The *Hotel Lido*, Consulado 26 entre Animas y

Trocadero, has one PC, US$6 per hr, but it is frustratingly slow. Prepaid *Etecsa* cards can be used in the International Press Center on La Rampa, Vedado, where there are also long queues. Several post offices have computers for the *Telecorreos* prepaid cards. These include the post office under the Ministerio de Comunicaciones on Plaza de la Revolución (5 terminals, US$4.50 per 3 hrs, 0800-1940 daily, 24-hr service planned with more terminals, long queues, sometimes of over an hour, popular with students, snack bar, clean toilets), and the post office at Línea y Paseo (same prices, 24-hr service also proposed here, 8 terminals, good equipment).

Language schools

At the Faculty of Modern Languages at the University of Havana, courses start on the first Mon of the month with 20 hrs' study a week, Mon-Fri 0900-1300, US$250 for two weeks, US$650 full board. There are different levels of study and Cuban cultural courses are also available. A Spanish and popular dance course is US$300 for three weeks or US$670 full board. Spanish and Cuban Culture for six months is US$1,425 course only, and US$4,692 full board. Contact Dr Jorge Núñez Jover or Lic Ileana Dopico Mateo, Dirección Postgrado, Calle J Pt 556 entre 25 y 27, Vedado, T 334163/334245, F 335774, dpg@comuh.uh.cu

Medical facilities

The **Cira García Clinic**, 20 4101 esquina 41, Miramar, T 2042811/14, F 2041633. Payment in dollars, also the place to go for emergency dental treatment, the pharmacy (open 24 hrs) sells prescription and patent drugs and supplies that are often unavailable in other pharmacies, as does the **Farmacia Internacional**, Av 41 esquina 20, Miramar, T 2045051. Mon-Fri 0900-1700, Sat 0900-1200. **Camilo Cienfuegos Pharmacy**, L y 13, Vedado, T 333599. Daily 0800-2000. **Optica Miramar**, 43 1803 entre 18 y 18A, T 2042590, ophthalmology consultants, contact lenses, glasses. All hotels have a doctor on permanent duty, US$25 per consultation.

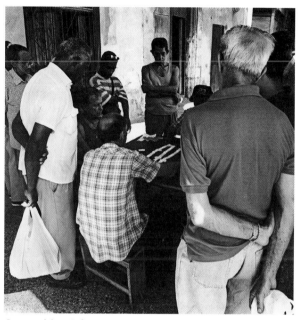

Competitive Cubans
Habaneros' favourite national pastimes – dominoes and baseball – are played out with competitive zeal on the back streets of La Habana Vieja.

Media
Newspapers *Granma*, available mornings except Sun and Mon; *Trabajadores*, Trade Union weekly; *Tribuna* and *Juventud Rebelde*, also weekly. *Opciones* is a weekly national and international trade paper. *Granma* also has a weekly edition, *Granma International*, in Spanish, English, French and Portuguese, and a monthly selected German edition; all have versions on the internet, www.granma.cu

Television There are two national channels: *Cubavisión* and *Tele Rebelde*, which broadcast morning and evening. The *Sun Channel* can be seen at hotels and broadcasts a special programme for tourists 24 hours a day. Some of the upmarket hotels also have satellite TV so you can catch up with CNN in Spanish or English.

Radio *Radio Habana Cuba*, 106.9 FM, multilingual, news and information. *Radio Musical Nacional*, 590MW/99.1 FM, classical music. *Radio Progreso*, 640MW/90.3 FM, music and drama. *Radio Rebelde*, 670 and 710MW/96.7 FM, current affairs, sport, music. *Radio Reloj*, 950MW/101.5 FM, 24-hr news station. *Radio Taíno*, 1290MW/93.2-93.4 FM, Cuban music with items of tourist interest.

Police

The main police station is at Dragones entre Lealtad y Escobar, Centro, T 624412, but in an emergency T 820116.

Post offices and courier services

Hotels and post offices charge for stamps in dollars, making them very expensive. They should be 45 centavos for a postcard to Europe and 75 centavos for a letter to Europe. Some postcards are now sold with postage included, look for the ones with the airmail stripe on the side. Post offices include Oficios 102, opposite La Lonja; on Ejido, next to the railway station; under the Gran Teatro de La Habana; in the *Hotel Nacional*, *Hotel Plaza* (5th floor, open 0700-1900) and in the *Hotel Habana Libre* building. For stamp collectors the **Círculo Filatélico** is on San José 1172 entre Infanta y Basarrata. Wed 1700-1900, Sat 1300-1700, Sun 0900-1200. Courier services are available. **Cubánacán Express** is a national and international courier service, Av 31 7230 esquina 41, Playa, T 2047848/2047960, F 2042499, cubex@courier.cha.cyt.cu **DHL**, Av 1 y 42, Miramar, T 331578, F 330999, and at Calzada 818 entre 2 y 4, Vedado, T 334351/2.

Public holidays

Liberation Day (1 January), Labour Day (1 May), Revolution Day (26 July and the day either side), Beginning of War of Independence (10 October) and Christmas Day (25 December). Other festive days that are not public holidays are 28 January (birth of José Martí 1853), 24 February (anniversary of renewal of War of Independence, 1895), 8 March (International Women's Day), 13 March (anniversary of 1957 attack on presidential palace in Havana by a group of young revolutionaries), 19 April (anniversary of defeat of mercenaries at Bay of Pigs, 1961), 30 July (martyrs of the Revolution day), 8 October (death of Che Guevara, 1967), 28 October (death of Camilo Cienfuegos, 1959), 27 November (death by firing squad of eight medical students by Spanish colonial government, 1871), 7 December (death of Antonio Maceo in battle in 1896).

Religious services

Places of worship   *Afrocuban*: Asociación Cultural Yoruba de Cuba, Prado 615 entre Monte y Dragones, La Habana Vieja, T 635953. 0900-1700. *Baptist*: J 555, Vedado, T 322250. *Buddhist*: Templo Dojo Soto, San Rafael esquina Aramburu, 1st floor, Apto 202, T 39421. Mon-Fri 0700-1900, from Sat 0800. *Islam*: Casa de los Arabes, Oficios 16 entre Obispo y Obrapía, La Habana Vieja, T 615868. *Jehovah's Witnesses*: Av 5 4608 entre 46 y 48, Playa. 0800-1800. Jewish, synagogue and community centre: *Bet Shalomé Temple*, I esquina 13, Vedado, T 328953, F 333778. Fri 2000-2200, Sat 0800-1200. *Methodist*: K 502 entre 25 y 27, Vedado, T 617771. *Presbyterian*: Salud 218, Centro Habana, T 621219. *Roman Catholic*: Sagrado Corazón, Reina e Belascoín y Gervasio, Centro Habana; Iglesia del Carmen, Infanta entre Neptuno y Concordia, Centro Habana, and many others. *Seventh Day Adventist*: La Rosa 272, Facueras y Santa Catalina, T 411275.

Taxis

One of the cheapest companies is **Panataxi**, a call-out service,
T 555555, although also outside most hotels and at the airport.
Head office: Santa Ana entre Marino y Boyeros. T 555461.
Other companies include **Havanauto**, T 2042424; **Habanataxi**,
T 419600; **Transgaviota**. Head office: Calle 100 y 31,
T 2604650/2672727; **Taxi OK**, T 2049518-9. Head office: Calle 32
108, Varadero, T45 667341; **MiCar**, T 2042444, and **Fénix**,
T 639720. To hire an old American mobile see Taxis, Getting
Around, p28.

Telephone and fax

Phone code for Cuba: 00-53, 7 for Havana.
Ministerio de Comunicaciones, Av Rancho Boyeros entre 19 de
Mayo y 20 de Mayo, Plaza de la Revolución, T 810875/820087. The
Empresa Telecomunicaciones de Cuba (*Etecsa*) , Av 33 1427
entre 18 y 14, Miramar, T 332476, F 332504.
Cubacel Telefonía Celular, 28 510 entre 5 y 7, Miramar,
T 332222, F 331737. There is a plentiful supply of phone boxes all
over the city, taking coins or phone cards, and it is written on the
side whether they are for local, national or international calls.
Etecsa phonecards are in different denominations from US$10-50,
which are much cheaper for phoning abroad, for example US$2
per min to USA and Canada, US$2.60 per min to Central America
and the Caribbean, US$3.40 to South America, US$4 to Spain, Italy,
France and Germany and US$4.40 to the rest of the world. To
phone abroad, dial 119 followed by the country and regional codes
and number. No collect calls allowed. Faxes can be sent from
Telecorreos and *Etecsa* offices and major hotels.

Time

Eastern Standard Time, five hours behind GMT; Daylight Saving
Time, four hours behind GMT. However, Cuba does not always
change its clocks the same day as the USA or the Bahamas.

Best to check in the spring and autumn so that you are not caught out with missed flights and buses etc.

Toilets

Hotels will always have toilets somewhere near the reception area; state-run restaurants will also have toilets for customers' use, but not all private restaurants have them; public toilets can be found in the centre of most towns, but you cannot rely on it.

Transport enquiries

Astro, Terminal de Omnibus Nacional, Boyeros y 19 de Mayo (3rd left via 19 de Mayo entrance), T 8703397. **Víazul**, Av 26 entre Av Zoológico y Ulloa, Nuevo Vedado, T 8811413, www.viazul.cu

Travel agents

Amistur, Paseo 406 entre 17 y 19, T 334544/662374/301220, F 553753, amistur@ceniai.inf.cu offers specialized visits to factories and schools as well as places of local historical or community interest. **Cuba Deportes**, Calle 29 710 entre 7 y 9, Miramar, T 2040945-7, F 2041914/2047230. Arranges all-inclusive sporting holidays. **Cubamar Viajes**, Paseo 306 entre 13 y 15, Vedado, T 662523-4, F 333111, cubamar@cubamar .mit.cma.net Some camping resorts, student groups and diving packages. **Cubanacán**, T 337952/330607, www.cubanacan.cu Offers birdwatching, scuba diving, hunting and fishing tours. **Gaviota Tours**, Hotels Kohly and El Bosque in Havana, T 2044781/294528/2047683, F 2049470, gavitour@gavitur.gav. cma.net Tours of the Oriente recommended (includes two nights in Hotel Porto Santo, Baracoa). **Havanatur**, Edif Sierra Maestra, Av 1 entre 0 y 2, Miramar, T 247416/249580, F 242074/242877. Also branches in many hotels, recommended for independent travellers who want tailor-made, but reasonably priced tours. **Horizontes**, Calle 23 156 entre N y O, Vedado, T 662004/662160, F 334585/553914, www.horizontes.cu, run hotels and activities for

Directory

'eco' tourists and hunters. Fly-drive tours can be arranged. **Islazul**, Malecón y G, Vedado, T 325152/320571-85, F 333458/324410, cmazul@Teda.get.cma.net Previously for Cubans only, now also for foreigners, offering more unusual and off-the-beaten track excursions. **Rumbos**, Calle O 108 entre 1 y 3, Miramar, T 2049626-8, F2047167/2049626, director@rumvia.rumb.cma. net Organizes excursions and runs bars and cafés. **Sol y Son**, Calle 23 64, La Rampa, Vedado, T 333271/335159, F 333385. The travel company of *Cubana* airline.

A sprint through history

1508	Sebastián de Ocampo circumnavigates Cuba.
1511	Diego de Velázquez conquers Cuba.
1526	African slaves are imported as Amerindians die out because of disease and murder. Plantation agriculture begins with sugar, then tobacco (17th century) and coffee (18th century).
1762	The British capture Havana and hold it until it is exchanged for Florida in 1763.
1868	10-year First War of Independence. Carlos Manuel de Céspedes, a creole landowner, issues a proclamation of independence, while simultaneously freeing his slaves. General Antonio Maceo and Máximo Gómez are heroes from this time.
1878	US interests begin to take over sugar plantations and Cuba becomes dependent on the US market.
1895	Second War of Independence. Led by poet and revolutionary, José Martí, with Maceo and Gómez.
1898	The US battleship *Maine* explodes in Havana harbour and the USA declares war on Spain to protect its Cuban investments. Spain is defeated. Peace is signed and US forces occupy Cuba.
1902	Republic of Cuba is proclaimed. The Platt Amendment to the Constitution, makes Cuba a US protectorate. The Americans retain naval bases at Río Hondo and Guantánamo Bay.
1924	Gerardo Machado is elected president on a wave of popularity but an economic downturn leads to strikes, which he represses.

1928	Machado 'persuades' Congress to grant him a second term. Opposition is harshly repressed. Nationalists call a general strike in protest at US interference and Machado goes into exile.
1933	Fulgencio Batista stages a coup and holds power through presidential puppets.
1934	The Platt Amendment is repealed to quell growing unrest. The USA relinquishes the right to intervene but retains a 99-year lease on Guantánamo Bay.
1940-44	Batista is elected president. Corruption and violence continue.
1952	Batista stages a military coup. A harshly repressive dictatorship is installed.
1953	Fidel Castro and 160 revolutionaries attack the Moncada barracks in Santiago de Cuba on 26 July. The attack fails. Castro and his brother, Raúl, are tried and imprisoned.
1955	The Castro brothers are amnestied and go to Mexico, where they work on a nationalist revolutionary programme and meet Che Guevara.
1956	The Castros with 82 others land in eastern Cuba and begin a military campaign in the Sierra Maestra, which spreads throughout the country.
1959	Batista flees the country on 1 January. Castro enters Havana and takes control of the island.
1960	Officials of the Batista régime are tried and executed. Sugar mills, oil refineries and foreign banks are nationalized, US property expropriated,

the judiciary and trade unions lose their independence, freedom of the press is abolished and professionals begin a steady exodus to Florida. Diplomatic relations are established with the USSR and the USA imposes a trade embargo.

1961   The USA severs diplomatic relations and attempts to isolate Cuba. The Bay of Pigs CIA-backed invasion is a fiasco. The Cuban Revolution is confirmed socialist.

1962   The Cuban Missile Crisis. Castro requests Soviet short-range missiles to deter invasion, but Kruschev sends medium-range missiles, capable of striking anywhere in the USA. JF Kennedy orders Soviet ships heading for Cuba to be stopped and searched in international waters. Kruschev eventually backs down and withdraws the missiles from Cuba.

1965   Cuban Communist Party is founded. Cuba becomes dependent on the USSR for economic survival with widespread subsidies.

1971   Political and intellectual opponents, religious believers and homosexuals are persecuted.

1980   Peruvian Embassy is overrun by 11,000 asylum-seekers. Castro allows a mass departure of 125,000 dissidents, including prisoners, homosexuals and mental patients who head for Miami.

1989   The collapse of the Eastern bloc nearly brings about Castro's downfall: 90% of Cuba's trade was with centrally-planned economies and Soviet aid was estimated at 25% of Cuba's GNP.

1990	The 'Special Period' (1990-94). Rationing is increased; petrol is scarce. GDP falls by 35% (1990-93). Exports fall from US$8.1bn (1989) to US$1.7bn (1993).
1994	Economic frustration boils over and 30,000 Cubans flee to Florida in one month. The USA is forced to accept 20,000 Cubans a year, while Castro agrees to prevent further departures.
1995	The government liberalizes the economy, allowing limited self-employment. Foreign investment is sought and tourism is actively promoted.
1996	Cuba shoots down two light aircraft piloted by Miami emigrés, allegedly over Cuban air space. President Clinton tightens US embargo.
1997	A spate of bombings in Havana targets the tourist industry. It is alleged the Miami-based Cuban American National Foundation is behind them.
1998	The Pope visits Cuba for the first time. He preaches against its human rights' record and abortion and condemns the US trade embargo preventing food and medicines reaching Cuba.
2001	A severe hurricane and a slowdown in tourism after 11 September leads to the worst financial crisis since 1989. The first commercial export of food from the USA arrives in Cuba.
2002	Former US President Jimmy Carter visits Cuba calling for an end to the embargo. The failure of the sugar industry forces Cuba to reduce the amount of land devoted to sugar by 60%.

Architecture

16th century	The most important architectural works were the forts built to guard Spain's valuable colony from pirate attack including the Castillo de la Real Fuerza overlooking the entrance to Havana's harbour.
17th century	Defensive construction continued with the building of the Castillo del Morro and the city walls. One and a half metres thick and 10 m high, they ran for nearly 5,000 m around the edge of the bay. A few fragments remain at Calle Egido y Avenida del Puerto.
18th century	The increased power enjoyed by the church in the 17th and 18th centuries led to many churches being built. The first baroque church in Havana, Iglesia de Nuestra Señora de Belén, was completed in 1718 on Calle Compostela. San Francisco de Asís was rebuilt in the baroque style in 1730. The baroque cathedral was completed in 1777. Colonial houses were typically Sevillian style: large, airy rooms on the first floor surrounded the central patio, the ground floor was reserved for warehouses and shops, and the *entresol*, between the ground and first floors, was where the slaves lived. Intricate carved *rejas* adorned the windows, and half-doors set with coloured glass divided the rooms. A good example is Casa de La Obra Pía.
19th century	The first neoclassical building was the Templete. In the early 1800s the cathedral had its baroque altars replaced with neoclassical ones. Many elaborate country houses were built outside the city walls, with inlaid marble floors, fountains and wrought-iron *rejas* typical of the neoclassical period.

1910-40	One of the most notable art nouveau buildings is the Palacio Velasco, built in 1912 on Capdevila esquina Agramonte in Centro. The best art deco is the Edificio Bacardí on Av de las Misiones, built in 1929 by the founder of Bacardi rum. The neo-renaissance Casino Español, now the Palacio de Los Matrimonios, is on Paseo de Martí (Prado).
1950	Aquiles Capablanca was the most popular architect of the 1950s. His Tribunal de Cuentas is one of the most admired 20th-century buildings in Latin America. He also built the Office of the Comptroller, Plaza de la República. Both buildings feature brightly coloured murals by Amelia Peláez, see below. The *Tropicana* nightclub, built by Max Borges Jr in 1952, was another work of stunning originality: exotic, sinuous curves on the shell-like structure are combined with tropical vegetation and the architect's own sculptures.
Post-Revolution	The Revolution saw less construction of grand buildings as the government concentrated on providing housing in Soviet-style concrete blocks and eliminating slums. The School of Plastic Arts was started in 1961 by Ricardo Porro and completed after his defection by Vittorio Garatti in 1965; described as resembling a stretched-out woman's body, with breast-like domes and curved walkways. Another good example of post-Revolution creativity is the *Coppelia* ice cream parlour, by Mario Girona, completed in 1966. Emphasis is now on restoring colonial mansions.

Art

19th century

With the rise of the independence movement, painters moved away from what was fashionable in Spain and developed styles endemic to the island.

1900-40

Víctor Manuel's (1897-1969) 1924 painting *Gitana Tropical*, with its echoes of Cézanne and Gauguin, caused a sensation and symbolized the beginning of modernism in Cuban art. An avant-garde movement developed and the art magazine *Avance* made its appearance in 1927. US political and economic interference led to a new nationalism among artists and intellectuals, who looked to Afro-Cuban images for inspiration.

1940s

The decade of the 1940s belonged to Wilfredo Lam (1902-82), Cuba's most famous painter. His friends Picasso and André Bréton introduced him to primitive art. Lam blended synthetic cubism, African masks and surrealism to create an essentially Cuban vision. One of his contemporaries, Amelia Peláez (1896-1968), looked west for her inspiration, to the mural painting of Mexico, while René Portocarrero (1912-85) incorporated Afro-Cuban imagery into his big colourful paintings.

Post-Revolution

The Revolution had a strong influence on developments: the first national art school was founded in the early 1960s and in 1976 the Escuela Superior de Arte was founded. Raúl Martínez (1927-95) was the best-known of the Cuban Pop Artists. The imagery of Cuban Pop Art came from the ubiquitous faces of revolutionaries, seen on murals all over Cuba. The 1970s was the most difficult era for artists in Cuba, with many political restrictions on their work; of the few that made it past the censors, Flavio Garciandia was the most notable, producing paintings that mixed abstract and figurative styles.

1980-2000 Conceptual art emerged in the 1980s and many alternative groups were formed, such as *Artecalle* – street art. There was also the *Puré* group, the most important member being José Angel Toirac. Despite emigration of many artists, the art scene still flourished and everything was questioned and deconstructed. Some, like the sculptor Alejandro Aguilera, distorted patriotic symbols in a confrontational way. The 1990s saw the rise of performance art as a means of expression. Carlos Garaicoa is one of the bigger names in this field, along with Tania Bruguera. Many alternative galleries have sprung up with a return to painting. This reflects the economic need, during the Special Period, for artists to make saleable objects again, though it also has its conceptual roots in post-modernism.

Books

Politically and culturally, Cubans look to the 19th-century poet and freedom fighter, José Martí (1853-95), as one of their most influential writers. Unlike other modernist poets of his age, Martí rejected contemporary European literature and considered precolumbian culture more relevant to a Latin American poet. *Negrismo*, in the 1920s, created non-intellectual poetry based on African dance rhythms and Afro-Cuban culture.

The mulatto, Nicolás Guillén (1902-1989), whose work included *Motivos de son* (1930), incorporated African rhythms in his *son* poetry. After the Revolution he was made president of the Union of Cuban writers and the National Poet.

The major writers at the time of the Revolution were Virgilio Piñera (1914-79), Alejo Carpentier (1904-80) and poet José Lezama Lima (1910-76). The founder of magical realism, Carpentier's early novels are among the most highly rated in Latin American literature, including *Los Pasos Perdidos* (The Lost Steps, 1953) and *El Siglo de las Luces* (Explosion in a Cathedral, 1962).

Lezama Lima was one of the driving forces behind *criollismo* n the 1940s-1950s, but scandalized post-Revolution Cuba with his novel *Paradiso* (Paradise, 1966), a thinly disguised account of his homosexual experiences. His rebellious, apolitical stance is an inspiration to today's poets, who seek to create non-political poetry with a more spiritual dimension. In the 1960s -1970s, persecution forced many writers to flee, eg Guillermo Cabrera Infante to London, Severo Sarduy to France. Conflict between artistic creativity and the Revolution exploded in 1971 when Herberto Padilla won a literary prize. His book of satirical and questioning poems was blocked and he was imprisoned. One of the most famous dissident novelists was Reinaldo Arenas (1943-90). Dogged by security forces for most of his youth, he was imprisoned as a dissident and homosexual, and only published his novel *El mundo alucinado* (Hallucinations, 1971) by smuggling the manuscript out of Cuba.

Nowadays Cuban writers find it easier to express their ideas. Havana has a legally recognized literary group. There is also a new generation of Cuban American writers, whose parents fled in the 1960s, who are now discovering their roots.

Arenas, R, *Antes que Anochezca* (Before Night Falls), (1994), Viking. Autobiography of a homosexual growing up in Cuba post-1959.

Cabrera Infante, G, *Tres Tristes Tigres* (1967), Three Trapped Tigers, (trans 1971), Faber & Faber,1989. Highly amusing, a tableau of Havana's nightlife in the time of Batista.

Calvo Ospina, H, *Salsa! Havana Heat, Bronx Beat* (1995), Latin American Bureau. Development of modern salsa from the slave ships to New York cut-throat business, via son, jazz and chachacha.

Ferguson, J, *The Traveller's Literary Companion*, *The Caribbean*, (1997), In Print. Good introduction to literature and writings on Cuba.

García, C, *Dreaming in Cuban* (1982 and 1992), Knopf and Flamingo. A novel about three generations of women, the grandmother who stayed behind, the daughter who emigrated to the USA after the Revolution and the granddaughter, a punk, who returns to visit.

Greene, G, *Our Man in Havana* (1958), William Heinemann. Spy thriller set at the end of the Batista regime as the revolutionaries close in.

Gutiérrez, PJ, *Dirty Havana Trilogy* (trans Natasha Wimmer, 2001, Faber & Faber). Pedro Juan gives up his job as a reporter to re-educate himself in his attitude to life and what makes him happy, with the aim of taking nothing seriously. This involves lots of sex, drugs, rum, music and other good things in life, highly explicit and with insights into what makes Havana tick.

Lumsden, I, *Machos, Maricones and Gays, Cuba and Homosexuality* (1996), Temple University Press. Very readable account of the attitudes of Cubans towards gay people since the days of slavery.

Miller, T, *Trading with the Enemy: A Yankee Travels Through Castro's Cuba* (1996). Set in the early 1990s this is a sharply observed travelogue. Detailing Miller's encounters with Cuba's colourful cast from bartenders to baseball players, it steers away from political issues.

Roy, M, *Cuban Music* (2002) Latin American Bureau. Comprehensive and accessible, all you wanted to know about the historical and ethnic roots of Cuban music, the political dimension and the artists involved.

Musical roots

"[At] every moment of its history, Cuba elaborated a sonorous and lively folklore of surprising vitality, receiving, meshing, and transforming diverse contributions, all of which led to the creation of new and clearly defined genres." *Alejo Carpentier*

Son, the centrepiece of Cuban music, and the expression of the Cuban identity, hit Havana in the early 20th Century. Music mesmerised the city, as the seductive rhythms of son set hips shaking and pelvises gyrating along Vedado's boulevards and down the old town's alleyways. In the 1920s, sextet fever launched the global Latin boom, with son erupting across the dance halls in Paris and pulsating through the music halls of New York.

Son is testimony to the fact that innovation is Cuba's longest lasting tradition. With its syncretic beats, it has spawned a legacy of musical hybrids; danzón, rumba, and cha cha cha. With the success of the Wim Wender's masterpiece, Buena Vista Social Club, son received universal recognition and entered the mainstream. While hip new Grammy-winning bands, like Los Van Van, dominate the airwaves at home and abroad, the adoration of old time legends like Ibrahim Ferrer and Compay Segundo has reached divine proportions. Although it is increasingly rare, you can still catch Cuba's musical gods playing to impassioned audiences at venues throughout the city, when they are not playing the more lucrative international circuit, see p145.

Son   The centrepiece of Cuban music, played by old school musicians and by new bands, like *Los Van Van*. Son originated in rural Oriente where old songs from Spain combined with African call-and-response choruses. The syncopated notes of the guitar and *tres* (a guitar-like instrument) contributed to early styles such as the satirical *Guaracha*, the *Guajira*, including the famous '*Guajira Guantanamera*', and *Nengón*, which soon developed, with the addition of bongo, maracas and marimbula, into the style known as son Changüí. By the late 1920s, Ignacio Piñero had formed his *Septeto Nacional*, (a seven piece band, including guitars, percussion, brass, vocals, playing traditional Cuban music) which added a hot trumpet to the central rhythm of the clave.

Salsa   The 1930s marked the beginning of modern salsa with the development of Arsenio Rodriguez' Conjunto style. Conga drums, timbales (or 'Paila' – optional), piano and more trumpets were injected into the traditional *Septeto*. This 'big band' son made much of the final, wild call-and-response or *montuno* section of the song. The later *Descargas* were improvised jam sessions which had major influences on US jazz. The *tumbao* played by the *tumbadoras* is derived from rumba, so salsa combines elements of the most prominent traditions: son, danzón and rumba. The 'child' of son – Latin salsa – has returned to Cuba in style with Isaac Delgado, El Chévere de la Salsa.

Revolutionary rhapsody   During the1950s, Beny Moré emerged as *Sonero Mayor*, updating son with jazz, mambo and cha cha cha. Along with Celia Cruz, Miguel Cuní and Félix Chapottín, son was

Best hot recent CD releases

• Azúcar Negra, *Andar Andando*
• Danny Lozada Y Su Timba Cubana, *Tanto Le Pedí*
• Paulito FG, *Una Vez Más*
• Tumbao Habana, *Por Amor*
• Giraldo Piloto Y Klimax, *Oye Como Va.*

ensured a place in the early 1960s. Elio Revé spent the 1960s-1970s creating a modern Changüí, revived with the aid of bassist Juan Formell, who later founded Los Van Van. The new generation have continued to innovate with groups such as NG La Banda, while Adalberto Alvarez carries the torch for a more rootsy son.

Rumba While son was appearing in the countryside, an African rhythm, the *Yuka*, was joining forces with the Spanish *Décima* and livening up the ports of Havana and Matanzas. This came to be known as rumba. African rhythms were played on whatever came to hand. Characters such as *Mama'buela* were created in mime and singers commented on current events or battled with each other for honours. This Rumba de Cajón also involved the Yambú, where a couple would mime courtship. The more sexual dance form known as Guaguancó (still the main rumba style) demanded more rapid playing. Great rumberos emerged, such as Florencio Calle and Celeste Mendoza, as well as groups who specialized in rumba, such as the well-travelled Muñequitos de Matanzas, who used the rhythms of the Abakuá religion. Rumba is a playfully competitive art form, although not always so playful. The 'guapos', or 'hard guys', take it very seriously and people do get hurt, sometimes even killed. The rhythms have got faster, break dancing and karate moves have been incorporated. Rumberos sing about the special period; in this way, rumba survives as a reflection of street life.

Danzón The popular Típica orchestras, influenced by cornettist Miguel Faílde, added subtle African rhythms to European Contradanza, along with a call-and-response *montuno* section, almost creating a Cuban ragtime. The Orquesta Típica slowly changed, adding piano and further percussion, while the 1920s saw a new arrival, the Charanga Francesa, a style developed by groups such as Los Van Van. During the 1940s-1950s, Orestes López (Cachao) and violinist Enrique Jorrín created the new Mambo and Cha cha cha styles directly from danzón. These driving rhythms are still popular and were fundamental to the explosion of Latin music and dance worldwide.

Canción Habanera This is regarded as the first truly Cuban vocal style. Emerging in the 1830s it had its greatest exponent in Eduardo Sánchez. Another Canción style, involving a singer and guitar, was developed during the 19th century in by Pepe Sánchez. His simple, beautiful songs inspired Sindo Garay. The romantic style known as Bolero soon developed from canción. Realizing the potential for expression, musicians like Silvio Rodríguez, Sara González and Pablo Milanés created the Nueva Trova. Their songs reflect the path of the Revolution.

Who's who: a bluffer's guide to Cuban music

Nothing's constant in the tumultuous world of Timba. **NG La Banda** is still around but its popularity, if not the respect it commands, seems to be on the slide these days. The band hasn't released a CD under its own name since 1997, though it's kept busy in various guises. **El Tosco** has his finger in virtually every progressive musical pie, as producer, guest flautist, or in some other capacity. **Manolín, El Médico de la Salsa** has been trying to straddle the Cuba-Miami divide and is paying the consequences.

Again, this quintessential timbero has released nothing since 1997 though more for political reasons apparently. His three CDs are all classics. **La Charanga Habanera** has split following a lawless escapade during which members landed on stage from a helicopter smoking weed, and one or more of them dropped their draws. Oops. Possibly some acrimony there, but three new bands in their place, all with recent releases. They are: **David Calzado y su Charanga Habanera**, **Charanga Forever**, and **Danny Lozada y su Timba Cubana**. Three world class groups instead of one. **Giraldo Piloto y Klimax** released its third CD in 2000, its best yet. Klimax's music is becoming increasingly sophisticated under a lightweight veneer, and while it has made no impact in British dance clubs, it is highly regarded by musicians and most Cubans in the UK. Issac Delgado was one of NG's original singers. He is the smoothie in the raucous world of Timba. Regarded by one NYT writer as one of the world's greatest singers, his band complements him.

Bamboleo has been through some changes over the years in line-up and style. One ex-lead singer now lives in the UK; another has formed her own group **Azúcar Negra**, and has just released a first brilliant CD. **Sello LA** includes children of the world famous rumberos, '**Los Papines**' and has one release under its belt. Similarly to Klimax, a teen-pop surface is supported by the richest percussion and arrangement. Other good bands include **Manolito y su Trabuco**, **Paulito (Paulo) FG**, **Sabrosura Viva**, **Conexión Salsera**, **Tumbao Habana** . Many of the bands listed above sound so distinct that to an uninitiated ear it may be difficult to grasp what unites them. Covering the gamut here's a good starter menu: 5 Classic Timba CDs: NG La Banda, *En La Calle*; Manolín (El Médico), *De Buena Fé*; La Charanga Habanera, *Tremendo Delirio*; Conexión Salsera, *Muy Caliente Para Ti*; Sabrosura Viva, *A Partir De Hoy*.

Language

Pronunciation

The stress in a Spanish word conforms to one of three rules: 1) if the word ends in a vowel, or in n or s, the accent falls on the penultimate syllable (ventana, ventanas); 2) if the word ends in a consonant other than n or s, the accent falls on the last syllable (hablar); 3) if the word is to be stressed on a syllable contrary to either of the above rules, the acute accent on the relevant vowel indicates where the stress is to be placed (pantalón). Note that adverbs such as cuando, 'when', take an accent when used interrogatively: ¿cuándo?, 'when?' Cubans, like many other Latin Americans, often drop the letter S in the middle or end of the word, replacing it with a slight aspiration, eg dos becomes do'h, and espera becomes e'hpera.

Unless listed below consonants can be pronounced in Spanish as they are in English.

b, v Their sound is interchangeable and is a cross between the English 'b' and 'v', except at the beginning of a word or after 'm' or 'n' when it is like English 'b'

c Like English 'k', except before 'e' or 'i' when it is as the 's' in English 'sip'

g Before 'e' and 'i' it is the same as j

h When on its own, never pronounced

j As the 'ch' in the Scottish 'loch'

ll As the 'g' in English 'beige'; sometimes as the 'lli' in 'million'

ñ as the 'ni' in English 'onion'

rr Trilled much more strongly than in English

z As the 's' in English 'sip'

Greetings, courtesies

Good morning *Buenos días*

How are you? *¿Cómo está?/¿Cómo estás?*

Pleased to meet you *Mucho gusto/encantado/encantada*
What is your name? *¿Cómo se llama?*
I am called… *Me llamo…*
Excuse me/I beg your pardon/sorry *Permiso/Disculpe*
I do not understand *No entiendo*
Please speak slowly *Hable despacio por favor*
I don't speak Spanish *No hablo español*
Do you speak English? *¿Habla usted inglés?*
Go away! *¡Váyase! ¡Lárgate!*
Leave me alone *No me moleste*

Money
bill *la cuenta*
cheap *barato*
credit card *la tarjeta de crédito*
exchange house *la casa de cambio*, CADECA
expensive *caro*
How much does it cost? *¿Cuánto cuesta?*
travellers' cheques *los cheques de viajero*

Getting around
corner *la esquina*
between *entre*
How do I get to_? *¿Cómo llegar a_?*
on the left/right *a la izquierda/derecha*
straight on *derecho*
ticket office *la taquilla*
To walk *caminar*
When does the plane leave/arrive? *¿A qué hora sale/llega el avión?*
Where can I buy tickets? *¿Dónde se puede comprar boletos?*

Accommodation
Have you got a room for two people? *¿Tiene habitación para dos personas?*

Is service included? *¿Está incluído el servicio?*
clean/dirty towels *las toallas limpias/sucias*
pillows *las almohadas*
sheets *las sábanas*
shower *la ducha*
single/double *sencillo/doble*
to make up/clean *limpiar*
toilet paper *el papel higiénico*
with private bathroom *con baño*
with two beds *con dos camas*

Time

At half past two/two thirty *a las dos y media*
At a quarter to three *a las tres menos quince*
It's seven o'clock *son las siete*
It's twenty past six/six twenty *son las seis y veinte*
It's five to nine *son las nueve menos cinco*
In ten minutes *en diez minutos*
five hours *cinco horas*
Does it take long? *¿Tarda mucho?*
We will be back at… *Regresamos a las…*
What time is it? *¿Qué hora es?*
Monday *lunes*
Tuesday *martes*
Wednesday *miércoles*
Thursday *jueves*
Friday *viernes*
Saturday *sábado*
Sunday *domingo*

Food

avocado *el aguacate*
banana *el platanito, el guineo*
beans *los frijoles*

beef *la carne de res*
beef (shredded) *ropa vieja*
bread *el pan*
breakfast *el desayuno*
butter *la mantequilla*
cheese *el queso*
chicken *el pollo*
chilli pepper or green pepper *el ají*
egg *el huevo*
fish *el pescado*
garlic *el ajo*
ham *el jamón*
hot, spicy *picante*
ice cream *el helado*
lobster *la langosta*
lunch *el almuerzo*
meal, supper, dinner *la comida*
meat *la carne*
meatless *sin carne*
mixed salad *la ensalada mixta*
onion *la cebolla*
orange *la naranja*
paw paw, papaya *el mamey, el zapote*
plantain, green banana *el plátano*
pork *el cerdo*, (roast suckling pig) *Lechon asado*
potato *la papa*
prawns *los camarones*
raw *crudo*
rice (boiled) *el arroz blanco*
rice mixed with black beans, the national dish *Congris*
rice with kidney beans *Moros y cristianos* (Moors and Christians)
sandwich *el bocadillo/bocadito*
sugar *el azúcar*
sweet *dulce*

tenderloin *lomo*
Tuber (similar to sweet potato) *malanga*
turkey *pavo*
vegetables *los legumbres/vegetales*

Drink
beer *la cerveza*
cold *frío*
drink *la bebida*
drunk *borracho*
fruit milk shake *el batido*
hot *caliente*
ice *el hielo*
juice *el jugo*
milk *la leche*
red/white wine *el vino tinto/blanco*
rum (aged) *el ron (añejo)*
fizzy drink *la gaseosa/cola*
water (carbonated/still) *el agua (con/sin gas)*
white coffee *el café con leche*

Glossary

cuenta propista Self-employed
jinetero One who rides (like a jockey) on the back of tourists for cash
habaneros Havana residents
La Lucha The struggle (the Cuban tragi-comic response to a life of communist austerity)
paladar Home-cum-restaurant, courtesy of entrepreneurial *habaneros*
picante spicey
piropo flirtatious remark (in the street... from the charming to the obscene)

Index

Acknowledgements

Caroline would like to thank all those who helped out with the research of this guide. In Havana, many thanks to Cecilia Ercila Argüellas at Casa de la Américas; Elias at Callejón Hamel for donating his Sundays; the hospitality of Tommy Reyes; to Marilys and Miguel for great conversation and copious Cuba Libres; the generosity of Jorge Potts and Marilys; to Rigoberto Mena, Luis Barroso and Ian Meiklejohn, for informing and inspiring on contemporary Cuban art, and other cultural conundrums; to the attentive Luis at MILA. In New York, big thanks to fellow Latin travel *compañeras* Miranda and Beth, and Ruth Suarez in Seattle. Thanks to Lee Woolcock for the great Havana shots.

In the UK, special thanks to my family for infecting me with the Latin bug at an early age, and their support and encouragement, at home and abroad.

A big thanks to everyone at Footprint, especially office soprano Claire, for all her encouragement, patience and Cuban expertise, especially at the final stages; Stef, for all the support over the last year; and to Rachel Fielding for giving me the opportunity

Sarah Cameron would like to thank all those who wrote into the Cuba Handbook and to Simon Bull, cycling tour consultant with Blazing Saddles Travels. Thanks also due to Dave Willetts, Rufus Boulting-Vaughan and Mo Fini for music; Catherine Davies and Steve Wilkinson for cinema; Patrick Symmes for Che Guevara, Meic Haines for Afro Cuban religion. Information on Ernest Hemingway from Kenneth S Lynn's book *Hemingway* (Simon & Schuster, 1987).

Thanks also to Journey Latin America and South American Experience for flight information.

Credits

Footprint credits

Text editor: Claire Boobbyer
Series editor: Rachel Fielding

Production: Jo Morgan, Mark Thomas
In-house cartography: Sarah Sorensen,
Robert Lunn, Kevin Feeney

Proof-reading: Carol Franklin

Design: Mytton Williams
Maps: adapted from original cartography
by Netmaps SA, Barcelona, Spain

Photography credits

Front cover: Photonica
Inside: Lee Woolcock
Generic images: John Matchett
Back cover: Lee Woolcock

Print

Manufactured in Italy by Rotolito
Lombarda, Italy

Publishing information

Footprint Havana
1st edition
Text and maps © Footprint Handbooks
Ltd November 2002

ISBN 1 903471 49 4
CIP DATA: a catalogue record for this
book is available from the British Library

® Footprint Handbooks and the Footprint
mark are a registered trademark of
Footprint Handbooks Ltd

Published by Footprint Handbooks
6 Riverside Court
Lower Bristol Road
Bath, BA2 3DZ, UK
T +44 (0)1225 469141
F +44 (0)1225 469461
E discover@footprintbooks.com
W www.footprintbooks.com

Distributed in the USA by
Publishers Group West

Complete title list

Latin America & Caribbean

Latin America & Caribbean
Argentina
Barbados (P)
Bolivia
Brazil
Caribbean Islands
Central America & Mexico
Chile
Colombia
Costa Rica
Cuba
Cusco & the Inca Trail
Dominican Republic
Ecuador & Galápagos Handbook
Guatemala Handbook
Havana (P)
Mexico
Nicaragua
Peru
Rio de Janeiro
South American Handbook
Venezuela

North America

Vancouver (P)
Western Canada

Africa

Cape Town (P)
East Africa
Libya
Marrakech & the High Atlas
Morocco
Namibia
South Africa
Tunisia
Uganda

Middle East

Egypt
Israel
Jordan
Syria & Lebanon

Asia

Bali
Bangkok & the Beaches
Cambodia
Goa
India
Indian Himalaya
Indonesia
Laos
Malaysia
Myanmar (Burma)
Nepal
Pakistan
Rajasthan & Gujarat
Singapore
South India
Sri Lanka
Sumatra
Thailand
Tibet
Vietnam

Australasia

Australia
New Zealand
Sydney (P)
West Coast Australia

Europe

Andalucía
Barcelona
Berlin (P)
Bilbao (P)
Bologna (P)
Copenhagen (P)
Croatia
Dublin (P)
Edinburgh (P)
England
Glasgow
Ireland
London
Madrid (P)
Naples (P)
Northern Spain
Paris (P)
Reykjavik (P)
Scotland
Scotland Highlands & Islands
Spain
Turkey

(P) denotes pocket Handbook

For a different view…
choose a Footprint

Over 80 Footprint travel guides
Covering more than 145 of the world's most exciting
countries and cities in Latin America, the Caribbean, Africa, Indian
sub-continent, Australasia, North America, Southeast Asia, the
Middle East and Europe.

Discover so much more…
The finest writers. In-depth knowledge. Entertaining and accessible.
Critical restaurant and hotels reviews. Lively descriptions of all the
attractions. Get away from the crowds.

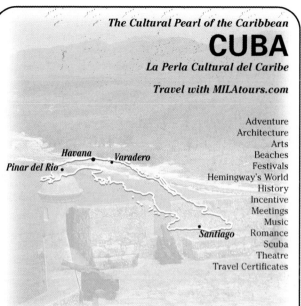

photo: www.rescio.net

Salsa and more

Latin CDs and Travel Agency

To the roots: Salsa, Spanish and Percussion

Classes + accomodation in **Havana**

Open 24 hours: Webshop with about 7000 CDs + 60000 audiofiles online

Quick delivery: about 4000 CDs in stock

Danza y Movimiento°...... www.dym.de

phone +49-40-340328 .... mail: info@dym.de
Danza y Movimiento GmbH .... Hütten 118 .... 20355 Hamburg - Germany

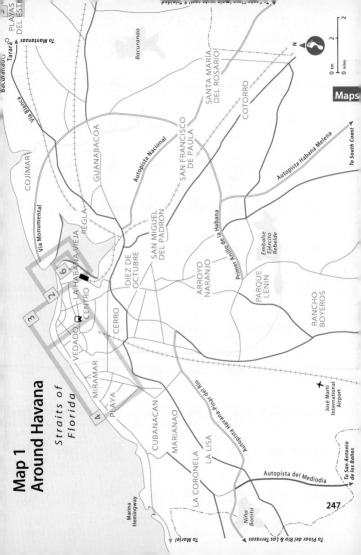

Map 1
Around Havana

Straits of Florida

To Matanzas
PLAYAS DEL ESTE
Tarará
Bacuranao
COJIMAR
Via Blanca
Via Monumental
GUANABACOA
REGLA
LA HABANA VIEJA
CENTRO
VEDADO
MIRAMAR
PLAYA
CUBANACAN
MARIANAO
LA CORONELA
LA LISA
Marina Hemingway
To Mariel

Bacuranao

SANTA MARIA DEL ROSARIO
COTORRO
SAN FRANCISCO DE PAULA
Autopista Nacional
SAN MIGUEL DEL PADRON
DIEZ DE OCTUBRE
CERRO
ARROYO NARANJO
Primer Anillo de la Habana
Embalse Ejército Rebelde
PARQUE LENIN
RANCHO BOYEROS
Autopista Habana Melena
To South Coast

Autopista Havana-Pinar del Río
José Martí International Airport
Autopista del Mediodia
To San Antonio de los Baños
Niña Bonita
To Pinar del Río & Las Terrazas

N

0 km 2
0 miles 2

Map 2 La Habana Vieja & Centro

Map symbols

✈ Airport
⊚ Police
⛴ Ferry
▣ Bus station
✚ Hospital
✉ Post office
Ⓜ Market
✝ Cathedral, church
🏛 Museum
Related map
Detail map

N

0 metres 200
0 yards 200

Straits of Florida

Castillo del Morro

Vía Monumental

Castillo de La Punta

(Malecón)

Ave. de Maceo

Calle San Lázaro

Calle Lea

Calle

Escobar

Gervasio

Virt

Belascoaín

Monumento General
Antonio Maceo

Calle Animas

lle Concordia

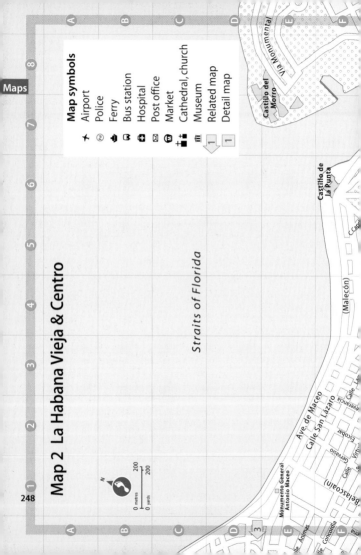

Bahía de la Habana

Fortaleza de San Carlos de la Cabaña

Cristo la Haba

Ave. Carlos Manuel de Céspedes (Avenida del Puerto)

Ferry Terminal to Casablanca/Regla

Convento de San Fco. de Asís

Pl. San Francisco de Asís

Castillo de la Real Fuerza

Pl. de Armas

Tacón

Mercaderes

Oficios

de Cuba

Chacón

Museo Nacional de la Música

Catedral de San Cristóbal

Pl. de la Catedral

LA HABANA VIEJA

Museo de la Revolución

Cuarteles

Tejadillo

Empedrado

San Juan de Dios

Calle Lamparilla

Calle Amargura

Plaza Vieja

Calle Santa Clara

Luz

Inquisidor

San Ignacio

Cuba

Ave. de las Misiones

Paseo de Martí (del Prado)

Calle del Morro

Agramonte (Zulueta)

Hotel Sevilla

Calle

Habana

Calle Obispo

O'Reilly

Compostela

Calle Teniente Rey (Brasil)

Calle Muralla

Convento de Santa Clara

Calle Sol

Calle Acosta

Jesús María

Calle Merced

Paseo de San Ignacio

Museo Nacional de Bellas Artes

Palacio de Bellas Artes

El Florida

Ave. Monserrate

Calle Villegas

Calle Bernaza

Calle del Cristo

Calle Obrapía

Calle Aguacate

Calle Picota

Calle Compostela

Hotel Inglaterra

Parque Central

Gran Teatro

San Martín (San José)

Paseo de Martí

Ave. de Bélgica (Egido)

Calle P. (Paula)

Casa Natal José Martí

Calle San Isidro

Calle Velázquez

Calle Desamparados

Ave. Italia (Galiano)

Calle Neptuno

San Miguel

San Rafael

Barcelona

The Capitolio

Calle Dragones

Parque Fraternidad

Calle Agramonte

Calle Economía

Calle Misión

Calle Arsenal

Estación Central de Ferrocarriles

Calle Florida

Calle Alambique

Calle San Nicolás

Antón Recio

Crespo

Consulado

Calle Blanco

Crespo

Trocadero

Calle Bernal

Calle Amistad

Calle Águila

Virtudes

Calle Neptuno

San Nicolás

Calle Manrique

Calle Campanario

CENTRO

Calle Salud

Ave. de Bolívar (Reina)

Calle Ángeles

Paseo

Partagás

Partagás

Calle Máximo Gómez (Monte)

Calle Corrales

Apodaca

Calle Gloria

Revillagigedo

Calle Esperanza

Cienfuegos

Aponte

Calle Suárez

Calle Factoría

Calle Florida

Main Police Station

Calle Zanja

Calle San Martín

Calle San Rafael

Calle San Miguel

Calle Neptuno

Escobar

Calle Condesa

de la Valla

Calle Estrella

Calle Maloja

Calle Indio

San Nicolás

Calle Aguila

Calle Revillagigedo

Calle Alcantarilla

Cerrada

Calle Puerta

Calle Diaria

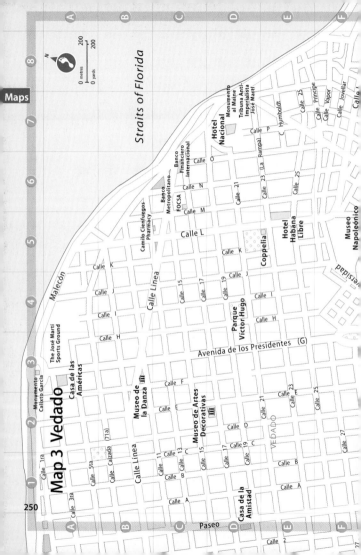

Map 3 Vedado

Straits of Florida

N

0 metres 200
0 yards 200

Monumento Calixto García

The José Marti Sports Ground

Casa de las Américas

Camilo Cienfuegos Pharmacy

Banco Metropolitano

FOCSA

Banco Financiero Internacional

Hotel Nacional

Monumento al Maine

Tribuna Anti-Imperialista José Martí

Museo Napoleónico

Hotel Habana Libre

Coppelia

Parque Victor Hugo

Avenida de los Presidentes (G)

Museo de la Danza

Museo de Artes Decorativas

VEDADO

Casa de la Amistad

Paseo

Malecón

Calle Linea

Calle Línea

Calle 5ta

Calle Calzada

Calle 1ra

Calle 3ra

(71a)

Calle 11

Calle 13

Calle 15

Calle 17

Calle 19

Calle 21

Calle 23

Calle 25

Calle 27

Calle A

Calle B

Calle C

Calle D

Calle E

Calle F

Calle H

Calle I

Calle J

Calle K

Calle L

Calle M

Calle N

Calle O

Calle P

Calle 2

Humboldt

Calle 25

Príncipe

Calle Vapor

Calle Jovellar

La Rampa

Maps

251

Map 4 Miramar

Straits of Florida

Malecón

Calle 1ra

Calle 3ra

Calle 5ta

Calle Calzada

Calle Línea

Parque
John Lennon

Casa de la
Amistad

Calle Zapata

Cementerio de Colón

Calle San Antonio Chiquito

C. Julia Borges

Teatro
Nacional

Ave. de la Loma

NUEVO VEDADO

Memorial
& Museo J.
Martí

Terminal de
Buses Viazul

Ave. de la Independéncia

253

Territorial

Map 5 Playas del Este

SANTA MARIA DEL MAR

Avenida de las Terrazas

Avenida del Sur

Avenida Primera

Via Blanca

Avenida de las Banderas

Avenida 3ª

Avenida de las Banderas

Avenida 9ª

Avenida Balcón

Strait

Casa de los Vinos y Quesos

Avenida Primera

Avenida Quinta

BOCA CIEJA

Via Blanca

Avenida de las Américas

Av. 13ª

0 metres	200
0 yards	200

Deportiva

Calle 13 de las Terrazas

Calle 14

Casa de los Vinos y Quesos

Itabo

Vía Blanca

Vía Blanca

5b

BOCA CIEGA

Avenida Prin

Avenida 6ª

Avenida 4ª

Avenida 4ª

SANTA MARIA DEL MAR

BOCA CIEGA GUANABO

5a

5b

f Florida

Avenida 1ª

Avenida 1ª A

Avenida 1ª

Avenida

Avenida 3ª

Avenida 5ª B

Avenida Quinta

Calle 500

Calle 502

Calle 504

Calle 492A

Calle 498A

Calle 490

Calle 492

Calle 494

Avenida 5ª D

Teatro Avenidas

Avenida Quinta

Parque de Diversiones

Calle 488A

Calle 496

Avenida 7ª

Calle 494A

Calle 500

Sta. Rosa de Lima

Calle 488

Calle 490 A

Avenida 9ª

Calle 484

Calle 486

Quito

Orlando Washington

Calle 477

Calle 474

Calle 474A

Calle 480

Calle 482

Avenida 9ª

Tegucigalpa

Calle 470

Calle 479

Vía 478

GUANABO

Calle 474A

Quebec

Calle 498

255 Calle G

Avenida 11ª

Avenida Mes

Calle 471

Avenida 11ª

Habana

Calle H

7 8 9 10 11 12

Map 6 La Habana Vieja

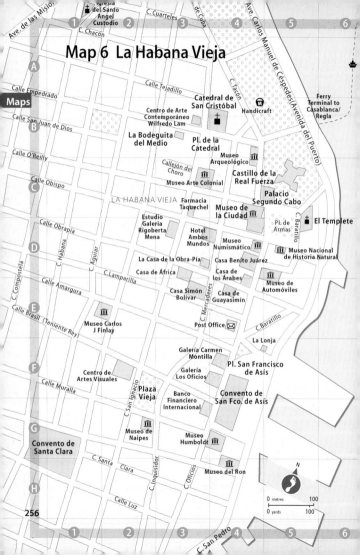

Ave. de las Misio

C.Cuarteles

C. de Cuba

Ave. Carlos Manuel de Céspedes(Avenida del Puerto)

Iglesia del Santo Angel Custodio

C. Chacón

Calle Empedrado

Calle Tejadillo

C.Tacón

Ferry Terminal to Casablanca/ Regla

Calle San Juan de Dios

Catedral de San Cristóbal

Handicraft

Maps

Centro de Arte Contemporáneo Wilfredo Lam

Calle O'Reilly

La Bodeguita del Medio

Pl. de la Catedral

Museo Arqueológico

Calle Obispo

Callejón del Choro

Castillo de la Real Fuerza

Museo Arte Colonial

Palacio Segundo Cabo

LA HABANA VIEJA

Farmacia Taquechel

Museo de la Ciudad

Pl. de Armas

El Templete

Calle Obrapía

Estudio Galería Rigoberta Mena

Hotel Ambos Mundos

Museo Numismático

Museo Nacional de Historia Natural

C. Habana

C. Aguiar

La Casa de la Obra-Pía

Casa Benito Juárez

Casa de África

C.Lamparilla

Casa de los Árabes

Museo de Automóviles

Calle Amargura

Casa Simón Bolívar

Casa de Guayasimín

C. Compostela

C. Mercaderes

Calle Brasil (Teniente Rey)

Museo Carlos J Finlay

Post Office

C. Baratillo

La Lonja

Galería Carmen Montilla

Centro de Artes Visuales

Galería Los Oficios

Pl. San Francisco de Asís

Calle Muralla

Plaza Vieja

Banco Financiero Internacional

Convento de San Fco. de Asís

C. San Ignacio

Museo de Naipes

Museo Humboldt

Convento de Santa Clara

C. Santa Clara

C.Inquisidor

C. Oficios

Museo del Ron

Calle Luz

N

0 metres 100

0 yards 100

256

C. San Pedro